www.EffortlessMath.com

... So Much More Online!

✓ FREE Math lessons

✓ More Math learning books!

✓ Mathematics Worksheets

✓ Online Math Tutors

Need a PDF version of this book?

Please visit www.EffortlessMath.com

5 CBEST
Math Practice
Tests

Extra Practice to Help Achieve an Excellent Score

By

Reza Nazari

All inquiries should be addressed to:
info@effortlessMath.com
www.EffortlessMath.com

ISBN: 978-1-63719-076-0

Published by: **Effortless Math Education Inc.**

For Online Math Practice Visit www.EffortlessMath.com

Welcome to

CBEST Math Prep 2021

Thank you for choosing Effortless Math for your CBEST Math test preparation and congratulations on making the decision to take the CBEST test! It's a remarkable move you are taking, one that shouldn't be diminished in any capacity. That's why you need to use every tool possible to ensure you succeed on the test with the highest possible score, and this extensive practice book is one such tool.

If math has never been a strong subject for you, **don't worry**! This book will help you prepare for (and even ACE) the CBEST test's math section. As test day draws nearer, effective preparation becomes increasingly more important. Thankfully, you have this comprehensive practice book to help you get ready for the test. With this book, you can feel confident that you will be more than ready for the CBEST Math test when the time comes.

First and foremost, it is important to note that this book is a practice book and not a prep book. Every test of this "self-guided math practice book" was carefully developed to ensure that you are making the most effective use of your time while preparing for the test. This up-to-date guide reflects the 2021 test guidelines and will put you on the right track to hone your math skills, overcome exam anxiety, and boost your confidence, so that you can have your best to succeed on the CBEST Math test.

This practice book will:

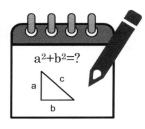

☑ Explain the format of the CBEST Math test.

☑ Describe specific test-taking strategies that you can use on the test.

☑ Provide CBEST Math test-taking tips.

☑ Help you identify the areas in which you need to concentrate your study time.

☑ Offer CBEST Math questions and explanations to help you develop the basic math skills.

☑ Give **realistic and full-length practice tests** (featuring new question types) with detailed answers to help you measure your exam readiness and build confidence.

This practice book contains 5 practice tests to help you succeed on the CBEST Math test. You'll get in-depth instructions on every math topic as well as tips and techniques on how to answer each question type. You'll also get plenty of practice questions to boost your test-taking confidence.

In addition, in the following pages you'll find:

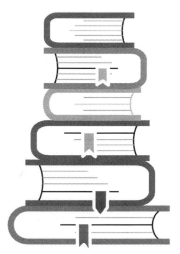

➤ **How to Use This Book Effectively** – This section provides you with step-by-step instructions on how to get the most out of this comprehensive practice book.

➤ **How to study for the CBEST Math Test** – A six-step study program has been developed to help you make the best use of this book and prepare for your CBEST Math test. Here you'll find tips and strategies to guide your study program and help you understand CBEST Math and how to ace the test.

➢ **CBEST Math Review** – Learn everything you need to know about the CBEST Math test.

➢ **CBEST Math Test-Taking Strategies** – Learn how to effectively put these recommended test-taking techniques into use for improving your CBEST Math score.

➢ **Test Day Tips** – Review these tips to make sure you will do your best when the big day comes.

Effortless Math's CBEST Online Center

Effortless Math Online CBEST Center offers a complete study program, including the following:

✓ Step-by-step instructions on how to prepare for the CBEST Math test

✓ Numerous CBEST Math worksheets to help you measure your math skills

✓ Complete list of CBEST Math formulas

✓ Video lessons for all CBEST Math topics

✓ Full-length CBEST Math practice tests

✓ And much more...

No Registration Required.

Visit **EffortlessMath.com/CBEST** to find your online CBEST Math resources.

How to Use This Book Effectively

Look no further when you need a practice book to improve your math skills to succeed on the math portion of the CBEST test. Each section of this comprehensive practice book will provide you with the knowledge, tools, and understanding needed to succeed on the test.

It's imperative that you understand each practice question before moving onto another one, as that's the way to guarantee your success. Each practice test provides you with a step-by-step guide of every question to better understand the content that will be on the test. To get the best possible results from this book:

➢ **Begin studying long before your test date**. This provides you ample time to learn the different math concepts. The earlier you begin studying for the test, the sharper your skills will be. Do not procrastinate! Provide yourself with plenty of time to learn the concepts and feel comfortable that you understand them when your test date arrives.

➢ **Practice consistently**. Study CBEST Math concepts at least 20 to 30 minutes a day. Remember, slow and steady wins the race, which can be applied to preparing for the CBEST Math test. Instead of cramming to tackle everything at once, be patient and learn the math topics in short bursts.

➢ Whenever you get a math problem wrong, **mark it off, and review it later** to make sure you understand the concept.

➢ Once you've reviewed the book's instructions, **take a practice test** to gauge your level of readiness. Then, review your results. Read detailed answers and solutions for each question you missed.

➢ **Take another practice test** to get an idea of how ready you are to take the actual exam. Taking the practice tests will give you the confidence you need on test day. Simulate the CBEST testing environment by sitting in a quiet room free from distraction. Make sure to clock yourself with a timer.

How to Study for the CBEST Math Test

Studying for the CBEST Math test can be a really daunting and boring task. What's the best way to go about it? Is there a certain study method that works better than others? Well, studying for the CBEST Math can be done effectively. The following six-step program has been designed to make preparing for the CBEST Math test more efficient and less overwhelming.

Step 1 - Create a study plan
Step 2 - Choose your study resources
Step 3 - Review, Learn, Practice
Step 4 - Learn and practice test-taking strategies
Step 5 - Learn the CBEST Test format and take practice tests
Step 6 - Analyze your performance

STEP 1: Create a Study Plan

It's always easier to get things done when you have a plan. Creating a study plan for the CBEST Math test can help you to stay on track with your studies. It's important to sit down and prepare a study plan with what works with your life, work, and any other obligations you may have. Devote enough time each day to studying. It's also a great idea to break down each section of the exam into blocks and study one concept at a time.

It's important to understand that there is no "right" way to create a study plan. Your study plan will be personalized based on your specific needs and learning style.

Follow these guidelines to create an effective study plan for your CBEST Math test:

★ **Analyze your learning style and study habits** – Everyone has a different learning style. It is essential to embrace your individuality and the unique way you learn. Think about what works and what doesn't work for you. Do you prefer CBEST Math prep books or a combination of textbooks and video lessons? Does it work better for you if you study every night for thirty minutes or is it more effective to study in the morning before going to work?

★ **Evaluate your schedule** – Review your current schedule and find out how much time you can consistently devote to CBEST Math study.

★ **Develop a schedule** – Now it's time to add your study schedule to your calendar like any other obligation. Schedule time for study, practice, and review. Plan out which topic you will study on which day to ensure that you're devoting enough time to each concept. Develop a study plan that is mindful, realistic, and flexible.

★ **Stick to your schedule** – A study plan is only effective when it is followed consistently. You should try to develop a study plan that you can follow for the length of your study program.

★ **Evaluate your study plan and adjust as needed** – Sometimes you need to adjust your plan when you have new commitments. Check in with yourself regularly to make sure that you're not falling behind in your study plan. Remember, the most important thing is sticking to your plan. Your study plan is all about helping you be more productive. If you find that your study plan is not as effective as you want, don't get discouraged. It's okay to make changes as you figure out what works best for you.

STEP 2: Choose Your Study Resources

There are numerous textbooks and online resources available for the CBEST Math test, and it may not be clear where to begin. Don't worry! Effortless Math's CBEST online center provides everything you need to fully prepare for your CBEST Math test. In addition to the practice tests in this book, you can also use Effortless Math's online resources. (video lessons, worksheets, formulas, etc.)

Simply visit EffortlessMath.com/CBEST to find your online CBEST Math resources.

STEP 3: Review, Learn, Practice

Effortless Math's CBEST course breaks down each subject into specific skills or content areas. For instance, the percent concept is separated into different topics— percent calculation, percent increase and decrease, percent problems, etc. Use our online resources to help you go over all key math concepts and topics on the CBEST Math test.

As you review each concept, take notes or highlight the concepts you would like to go over again in the future. If you're unfamiliar with a topic or something is difficult for you, do additional research on it. For each math topic, plenty of instructions, step-by-step guides, and examples are provided to ensure you get a good grasp of the material. You can also find video lessons on the <u>Effortless Math website</u> for each CBEST Math concept.

Quickly review the topics you do understand to get a brush-up of the material. Be sure to use the worksheets and do the practice questions provided on the Effortless Math's online center to measure your understanding of the concepts.

STEP 4: Learn and Practice Test-taking Strategies

In the following sections, you will find important test-taking strategies and tips that can help you earn extra points. You'll learn how to think strategically and when to guess if you don't know the answer to a question. Using CBEST Math test-taking strategies and tips can help you raise your score and do well on the test. Apply test taking strategies on the practice tests to help you boost your confidence.

STEP 5: Learn the CBEST Test Format and Take Practice Tests

The CBEST *Test Review* section provides information about the structure of the CBEST test. Read this section to learn more about the CBEST test structure, different test sections, the number of questions in each section, and the section time limits. When you have a prior understanding of the test format and different types of CBEST Math questions, you'll feel more confident when you take the actual exam.

Once you have read through the instructions and lessons and feel like you are ready to go – take advantage of the full-length CBEST Math practice tests available in this book. Use the practice tests to sharpen your skills and build confidence.

The CBEST Math practice tests offered in the book are formatted similarly to the actual CBEST Math test. When you take each practice test, try to simulate actual testing conditions. To take the practice tests, sit in a quiet space, time yourself, and work through as many of the questions as time allows. The practice tests are followed by detailed answer explanations to help you find your weak areas, learn from your mistakes, and raise your CBEST Math score.

STEP 6: Analyze Your Performance

After taking the practice tests, look over the answer keys and explanations to learn which questions you answered correctly and which you did not. Never be discouraged if you make a few mistakes. See them as a learning opportunity. This will highlight your strengths and weaknesses.

You can use the results to determine if you need additional practice or if you are ready to take the actual CBEST Math test.

Looking for more?

Visit <u>EffortlessMath.com/CBEST</u> to find hundreds of CBEST Math worksheets, video tutorials, practice tests, CBEST Math formulas, and much more.

Or scan this QR code.

No Registration Required.

CBEST Test Review

The California Basic Educational Skills Test (CBEST) is a computer-based test for Educators who want to gain credentials and teach at public schools. In essence, it is a broad and quick assessment of test takers' academic abilities.

The exam was designed and is administered by the California legislation. The CBEST test contains three sections.

- Math
- Reading
- Writing

CBEST does not test an individual's teaching abilities; it only measures reading skills (comprehension, analysis, and research skills), mathematics skills (calculations and problem solving, etc.), and writing skills that are vital in the education field, either at the elementary, secondary, or higher education levels.

The CBEST Math is comprised of 50 multiple choice questions and test takers have 4 hours to complete all three sections. You may take 1, 2, or all 3 sections in a single test session; you do not have to pass all 3 sections at a single administration.

Use of calculators is prohibited on this examination.

CBEST Mathematics cover the following topics:

- Estimation, measurement, and statistical principles (30%)
- Computation and problem solving (35%)
- Numerical and graphic relationships (35%)

CBEST Math Test-Taking Strategies

Here are some test-taking strategies that you can use to maximize your performance and results on the CBEST Math test.

#1 : USE THIS APPROACH TO ANSWER EVERY CBEST MATH QUESTION

- Review the question to identify keywords and important information.

- Translate the keywords into math operations so you can solve the problem.

- Review the answer choices. What are the differences between answer choices?

- Draw or label a diagram if needed.

- Try to find patterns.

- Find the right method to answer the question. Use straightforward math, plug in numbers, or test the answer choices (backsolving).

- Double-check your work.

#2 : USE EDUCATED GUESSING

This approach is applicable to the problems you understand to some degree but cannot solve using straightforward math. In such cases, try to filter out as many answer choices as possible before picking an answer. In cases where you don't have a clue about what a certain problem entails, don't waste any time trying to eliminate answer choices. Just choose one randomly before moving onto the next question.

As you can ascertain, direct solutions are the most optimal approach. Carefully read through the question, determine what the solution is using the math you have learned before, then coordinate the answer with one of the choices available to you. Are you stumped? Make your best guess, then move on.

Don't leave any fields empty! Even if you're unable to work out a problem, strive to answer it. Take a guess if you have to. You will not lose points by getting an answer wrong, though you may gain a point by getting it correct!

#3: BALLPARK

A ballpark answer is a rough approximation. When we become overwhelmed by calculations and figures, we end up making silly mistakes. A decimal that is moved by one unit can change an answer from right to wrong, regardless of the number of steps that you went through to get it. That's where ballparking can play a big part.

If you think you know what the correct answer may be (even if it's just a ballpark answer), you'll usually have the ability to eliminate a couple of choices. While answer choices are usually based on the average student error and/or values that are closely tied, you will still be able to weed out choices that are way far afield. Try to find answers that aren't in the proverbial ballpark when you're looking for a wrong answer on a multiple-choice question. This is an optimal approach to eliminating answers to a problem.

#4: BACKSOLVING

All questions on the CBEST Math test will be in multiple-choice format. Many test-takers prefer multiple-choice questions, as at least the answer is right there. You'll typically have five answers to pick from. You simply need to figure out which one is correct. Usually, the best way to go about doing so is "backsolving."

As mentioned earlier, direct solutions are the most optimal approach to answering a question. Carefully read through a problem, calculate a solution, then correspond the answer with one of the choices displayed in front of you. If you can't calculate a solution, your next best approach involves "backsolving."

When backsolving a problem, contrast one of your answer options against the problem you are asked, then see which of them is most relevant. More often than not, answer choices are listed in ascending or descending order. In such cases, try out the choices B or C. If it's not correct, you can go either down or up from there.

#5: Plugging In Numbers

"Plugging in numbers" is a strategy that can be applied to a wide range of different math problems on the CBEST Math test. This approach is typically used to simplify a challenging question so that it is more understandable. By using the strategy carefully, you can find the answer without too much trouble.

The concept is fairly straightforward–replace unknown variables in a problem with certain values. When selecting a number, consider the following:

- Choose a number that's basic (just not too basic). Generally, you should avoid choosing 1 (or even 0). A decent choice is 2.

- Try not to choose a number that is displayed in the problem.

- Make sure you keep your numbers different if you need to choose at least two of them.

- More often than not, choosing numbers merely lets you filter out some of your answer choices. As such, don't just go with the first choice that gives you the right answer.

- If several answers seem correct, then you'll need to choose another value and try again. This time, though, you'll just need to check choices that haven't been eliminated yet.

- If your question contains fractions, then a potential right answer may involve either an LCD (least common denominator) or an LCD multiple.

- 100 is the number you should choose when you are dealing with problems involving percentages.

CBEST Math – Test Day Tips

After practicing and reviewing all the math concepts you've been taught, and taking some CBEST mathematics practice tests, you'll be prepared for test day. Consider the following tips to be extra-ready come test time.

Before Your Test

What to do the night before:

- **Relax!** One day before your test, study lightly or skip studying altogether. You shouldn't attempt to learn something new, either. There are plenty of reasons why studying the evening before a big test can work against you. Put it this way–a marathoner wouldn't go out for a sprint before the day of a big race. Mental marathoners–such as yourself–should not study for any more than one hour 24 hours before a CBEST test. That's because your brain requires some rest to be at its best. The night before your exam, spend some time with family or friends, or read a book.

- **Avoid bright screens** - You'll have to get some good shuteye the night before your test. Bright screens (such as the ones coming from your laptop, TV, or mobile device) should be avoided altogether. Staring at such a screen will keep your brain up, making it hard to drift asleep at a reasonable hour.

- **Make sure your dinner is healthy** - The meal that you have for dinner should be nutritious. Be sure to drink plenty of water as well. Load up on your complex carbohydrates, much like a marathon runner would do. Pasta, rice, and potatoes are ideal options here, as are vegetables and protein sources.

- **Get your bag ready for test day** - The night prior to your test, pack your bag with your stationery, admissions pass, ID, and any other gear that you need. Keep the bag right by your front door.

- **Make plans to reach the testing site** - Before going to sleep, ensure that you understand precisely how you will arrive at the site of the test. If parking is something you'll have to find first, plan for it. If you're dependent on public transit, then review the schedule. You should also make sure that the train/bus/subway/streetcar you use will be running. Find out about road closures as well. If a parent or friend is accompanying you, ensure that they understand what steps they have to take as well.

The Day of the Test ....

- **Get up reasonably early, but not too early.**

- **Have breakfast** - Breakfast improves your concentration, memory, and mood. As such, make sure the breakfast that you eat in the morning is healthy. The last thing you want to be is distracted by a grumbling tummy. If it's not your own stomach making those noises, another test taker close to you might be instead. Prevent discomfort or embarrassment by consuming a healthy breakfast. Bring a snack with you if you think you'll need it.

- **Follow your daily routine** - Do you watch Good Morning America each morning while getting ready for the day? Don't break your usual habits on the day of the test. Likewise, if coffee isn't something you drink in the morning, then don't take up the habit hours before your test. Routine consistency lets you concentrate on the main objective—doing the best you can on your test.

- **Wear layers** - Dress yourself up in comfortable layers. You should be ready for any kind of internal temperature. If it gets too warm during the test, take a layer off.

- **Get there on time** - The last thing you want to do is get to the test site late. Rather, you should be there 45 minutes prior to the start of the test. Upon your arrival, try not to hang out with anybody who is nervous. Any anxious energy they exhibit shouldn't influence you.

- **Leave the books at home** - No books should be brought to the test site. If you start developing anxiety before the test, books could encourage you to do some last-minute studying, which will only hinder you. Keep the books far away—better yet, leave them at home.

- **Make your voice heard** - If something is off, speak to a proctor. If medical attention is needed or if you'll require anything, consult the proctor prior to the start of the test. Any doubts you have should be clarified. You should be entering the test site with a state of mind that is completely clear.

- **Have faith in yourself** - When you feel confident, you will be able to perform at your best. When you are waiting for the test to begin, envision yourself receiving an outstanding result. Try to see yourself as someone who knows all the answers, no matter what the questions are. A lot of athletes tend to use this technique—particularly before a big competition. Your expectations will be reflected by your performance.

During your test

- **Be calm and breathe deeply** - You need to relax before the test, and some deep breathing will go a long way to help you do that. Be confident and calm. You got this. Everybody feels a little stressed out just before an evaluation of any kind is set to begin. Learn some effective breathing exercises. Spend a minute meditating before the test starts. Filter out any negative thoughts you have. Exhibit confidence when having such thoughts.

- **Concentrate on the test** - Refrain from comparing yourself to anyone else. You shouldn't be distracted by the people near you or random noise. Concentrate exclusively on the test. If you find yourself irritated by surrounding noises, earplugs can be used to block sounds off close to you. Don't forget—the test is going to last several hours if you're taking more than one subject of the test. Some of that time will be dedicated to brief sections. Concentrate on the specific section you are working on during a particular moment. Do not let your mind wander off to upcoming or previous sections.

- **Skip challenging questions** - Optimize your time when taking the test. Lingering on a single question for too long will work against you. If you don't know what the answer is to a certain question, use your best guess, and mark the question so you can review it later on. There is no need to spend time attempting to solve something you aren't sure about. That time would be better served handling the questions you can actually answer well. You will not be penalized for getting the wrong answer on a test like this.

- **Try to answer each question individually** - Focus only on the question you are working on. Use one of the test-taking strategies to solve the problem. If you aren't able to come up with an answer, don't get frustrated. Simply skip that question, then move onto the next one.

- **Don't forget to breathe!** Whenever you notice your mind wandering, your stress levels boosting, or frustration brewing, take a thirty-second break. Shut your eyes, drop your pencil, breathe deeply, and let your shoulders relax. You will end up being more productive when you allow yourself to relax for a moment.

- **Review your answer.** If you still have time at the end of the test, don't waste it. Go back and check over your answers. It is worth going through the test from start to finish to ensure that you didn't make a sloppy mistake somewhere.

- **Optimize your breaks** - When break time comes, use the restroom, have a snack, and reactivate your energy for the subsequent section. Doing some stretches can help stimulate your blood flow.

After your test

- **Take it easy** - You will need to set some time aside to relax and decompress once the test has concluded. There is no need to stress yourself out about what you could've said, or what you may have done wrong. At this point, there's nothing you can do about it. Your energy and time would be better spent on something that will bring you happiness for the remainder of your day.

- **Redoing the test** - Did you pass the test? Congratulations! Your hard work paid off!

  If you have failed your test, though, don't worry! The test can be retaken. In such cases, you will need to follow the retake policy. You also need to re-register to take the exam again.

Contents

Time to Test

Time to refine your Math skill with a practice test

In this book, there are two complete CBEST Math Tests. Take these tests to simulate the test day experience. After you've finished, score your test using the answer keys.

Before You Start

- You'll need a pencil, a calculator and a timer to take the test.
- For each question, there are five possible answers. Choose which one is best.
- It's okay to guess. There is no penalty for wrong answers.
- After you've finished the test, review the answer key to see where you went wrong.

Good Luck!

CBEST Mathematics

Practice Test 1

2021-2022

Total number of questions: 50

Total time (Calculator): 90 Minutes

You may use a calculator on this practice test.

(On a real CBEST test, there is an onscreen calculator to use.)

1

Formula Sheet

Perimeter / Circumference

Rectangle

$Perimeter = 2(length) + 2(width)$

Circle

$Circumference = 2\pi(radius)$

Area

Circle

$Area = \pi(radius)^2$

Triangle

$Area = \frac{1}{2}(base)(height)$

Parallelogram

$Area = (base)(height)$

Trapezoid

$Area = \frac{1}{2}(base_1 + base_2)(height)$

Volume

Prism/Cylinder

$Volume = (area\ of\ the\ base)(height)$

Pyramid/Cone

$Volume = \frac{1}{3}(area\ of\ the\ base)(height)$

Sphere

$Volume = \frac{4}{3}\pi(radius)^3$

Length

1 foot = 12 inches

1 yard = 3 feet

1 mile = 5,280 feet

1 meter = 1,000 millimeters

1 meter = 100 centimeters

1 kilometer = 1,000 meters

1 mile ≈ 1.6 kilometers

1 inch = 2.54 centimeters

1 foot ≈ 0.3 meter

Capacity / Volume

1 cup = 8 fluid ounces

1 pint = 2 cups

1 quart = 2 pints

1 gallon = 4 quarts

1 gallon = 231 cubic inches

1 liter = 1,000 milliliters

1 liter ≈ 0.264 gallon

Weight

1 pound = 16 ounces

1 ton = 2,000 pounds

1 gram = 1,000 milligrams

1 kilogram = 1,000 grams

1 kilogram ≈ 2.2 pounds

1 ounce ≈ 28.3 grams

1) In five successive hours, a car traveled 40 km, 45 km, 50 km, 35 km and 55 km. In the next five hours, it traveled with an average speed of 65 $km\ per\ hour$. Find the total distance the car traveled in 10 hours.

    A. 425 km

    B. 450 km

    C. 550 km

    D. 600 km

    E. 1,000 km

2) How long does a 420-miles trip take moving at 50 miles per hour (mph)?

    A. 4 $hours$

    B. 6 $hours$ and 24 $minutes$

    C. 8 $hours$ and 24 $minutes$

    D. 8 $hours$ and 30 $minutes$

    E. 10 $hours$ and 30 $minutes$

3) What is the difference of smallest 5–digit number and biggest 5–digit number?

    A. 66,666

    B. 67,899

    C. 88,888

    D. 89,999

    E. 99,999

4) The arrow starts on space O and moves clockwise around the circle. It moves through one space each minute. What space will the arrow point to in 140 minutes?

    A. O

    B. P

    C. Q

    D. R

    E. S

5) Right triangle ABC has two legs of lengths 5 cm (AB) and 12 cm (AC). What is the length of the third side (BC)?

    A. 4 cm

    B. 6 cm

    C. 8 cm

    D. 13 cm

    E. 20 cm

6) What is 3.5% of 1,200?

    A. 900

    B. 600

    C. 300

    D. 60

    E. 42

7) Which of the following expressions is equivalent to $5x(4 + 2y)$?

    A. $x + 10xy$

    B. $5x + 5xy$

    C. $20xy + 2xy$

    D. $20x + 5xy$

    E. $20x + 10xy$

8) If $y = 5ab + 3b^3$, what is y when $a = 2$ and $b = 3$?

    A. 51

    B. 57

    C. 91

    D. 111

    E. 119

9) 15 is what percent of 20?

    A. 20%

    B. 25%

    C. 75%

    D. 150%

    E. 300%

10) The perimeter of the trapezoid below is 64. What s its area?

    A. $154 \ cm^2$

    B. $216 \ cm^2$

    C. $234 \ cm^2$

    D. $252 \ cm^2$

    E. $260 \ cm^2$

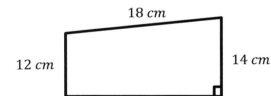

11) Two third of 15 is equal to $\frac{2}{5}$ of what number?

    A. 12
    B. 20
    C. 25
    D. 60
    E. 90

12) The marked price of a computer is D dollar. Its price decreased by 25% in January and later increased by 20% in February. What is the final price of the computer in D dollar?

    A. $0.80\ D$
    B. $0.82\ D$
    C. $0.90\ D$
    D. $1.20\ D$
    E. $1.40\ D$

13) What is the median of these numbers? $1, 10, 13, 8, 15, 18, 5$

    A. 8
    B. 10
    C. 13
    D. 15
    E. 20

14) The radius of a cylinder is 8 inches and its height is 14 inches. What is the surface area of the cylinder?

    A. $64\pi\ in^2$
    B. $128\pi\ in^2$
    C. $192\pi\ in^2$
    D. $256\pi\ in^2$
    E. $352\pi\ in^2$

15) The average of $13, 15, 20$ and x is 20. What is the value of x?

    A. 9
    B. 15
    C. 18
    D. 20
    E. 32

16) The price of a sofa is decreased by 25% to $450. What was its original price?

    A. $480

    B. $520

    C. $560

    D. $600

    E. $800

17) The area of a circle is 49π. What is the circumference of the circle?

    A. 7π

    B. 14π

    C. 32π

    D. 64π

    E. 124π

18) A $50 shirt now selling for $28 is discounted by what percent?

    A. 20%

    B. 44%

    C. 54%

    D. 60%

    E. 80%

19) From last year, the price of gasoline has increased from $1.40 per gallon to $1.75 per gallon. The new price is what percent of the original price?

    A. 72%

    B. 125%

    C. 140%

    D. 160%

    E. 180%

20) A boat sails 60 miles south and then 80 miles east. How far is the boat from its start point?

    A. 45 *miles*

    B. 50 *miles*

    C. 60 *miles*

    D. 70 *miles*

    E. 100 *miles*

21) Which of the following could be the product of two consecutive prime numbers?

  A. 2
  B. 10
  C. 14
  D. 20
  E. 35

22) Sophia purchased a sofa for $530.40. The sofa is regularly priced at $624. What was the percent discount Sophia received on the sofa?

  A. 12%
  B. 15%
  C. 20%
  D. 25%
  E. 40%

23) The score of Emma was half as that of Ava and the score of Mia was twice that of Ava. If the score of Mia was 40, what is the score of Emma?

  A. 10
  B. 15
  C. 20
  D. 30
  E. 40

24) A bag contains 18 balls: two green, five black, eight blue, a brown, a red and one white. If 17 balls are removed from the bag at random, what is the probability that a brown ball has been removed?

  A. $\frac{1}{2}$
  B. $\frac{1}{9}$
  C. $\frac{1}{6}$
  D. $\frac{16}{11}$
  E. $\frac{17}{18}$

25) The average of five consecutive numbers is 36. What is the smallest number?

  A. 38
  B. 36
  C. 34
  D. 12
  E. 8

26) The price of a car was $28,000 in 2012. In 2013, the price of that car was $18,200. What was the rate of depreciation of the price of car per year?

   A. 20%
   B. 30%
   C. 35%
   D. 40%
   E. 50%

27) The width of a box is one third of its length. The height of the box is one third of its width. If the length of the box is 36 cm, what is the volume of the box?

   A. 81 cm^3
   B. 162 cm^3
   C. 243 cm^3
   D. 1,728 cm^3
   E. 1,880 cm^3

28) If 60% of A is 30% of B, then B is what percent of A?

   A. 3%
   B. 30%
   C. 200%
   D. 300%
   E. 900%

29) How many possible outfit combinations come from four shirts, three slacks, and five ties?

   A. 11
   B. 14
   C. 15
   D. 30
   E. 60

30) An angle is equal to one ninth of its supplement. What is the measure of that angle?

   A. 8
   B. 9
   C. 10
   D. 18
   E. 19

31) If 40% of a class are girls, and 25% of girls play tennis, what percent of the class play tennis?

    A. 10%

    B. 15%

    C. 20%

    D. 40%

    E. 80%

32) How many tiles of $8\ cm^2$ is needed to cover a floor of dimension $7\ cm$ by $24\ cm$?

    A. 6

    B. 12

    C. 18

    D. 21

    E. 36

33) A rope weighs 600 grams per meter of length. What is the weight in kilograms of 14.2 meters of this rope? ($1\ kilogram = 1,000\ grams$)

    A. 0.0852

    B. 0.852

    C. 8.52

    D. 8.520

    E. 85.200

34) A chemical solution contains 6% alcohol. If there is $24\ ml$ of alcohol, what is the volume of the solution?

    A. $240\ ml$

    B. $400\ ml$

    C. $600\ ml$

    D. $1,200\ ml$

    E. $2,400\ ml$

35) The average weight of 18 girls in a class is $56\ kg$ and the average weight of 32 boys in the same class is $62\ kg$. What is the average weight of all the 50 students in that class?

    A. 50

    B. 59.84

    C. 61.68

    D. 61.90

    E. 62.20

36) The price of a laptop is decreased by 20% to $360. What is its original price?

    A. $320

    B. $380

    C. $400

    D. $450

    E. $500

37) Multiply and write the product in scientific notation:

$$(2.9 \times 10^6) \times (2.6 \times 10^{-5})$$

    A. 7.54×10

    B. 754×100

    C. 75.4×10^6

    D. 75.4×10^{-5}

    E. 7.54×10^{11}

38) If the height of a right pyramid is $14\ cm$ and its base is a square with side $6\ cm$. What is its volume?

    A. $432\ cm^3$

    B. $388\ cm^3$

    C. $236\ cm^3$

    D. $172\ cm^3$

    E. $168\ cm^3$

39) In a coordinate plane, triangle ABC has coordinates: $(-1, 4), (-2, 5)$, and $(5, 9)$. If triangle ABC is reflected over the y-axis, what are the coordinates of the new image?

    A. $(-1, -4), (-2, -5), (-5, -9)$

    B. $(-1, -4), (-2, -5), (5, -9)$

    C. $(-1, 4), (-2, 5), (5, 9)$

    D. $(1, 4), (2, 5), (5, 9)$

    E. $(1, 4), (2, 5), (-5, 9)$

40) Calculate the value of x for the right triangle shown below.

    A. $8\ ft$

    B. $10\ ft$

    C. $16\ ft$

    D. $18\ ft$

    E. $20\ ft$

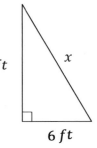

41) 11 yards 6 feet and 6 inches equals to how many inches?

   A. 348
   B. 354
   C. 470
   D. 474
   E. 482

42) 5 less than twice a positive integer is 73. What is the integer?

   A. 39
   B. 41
   C. 42
   D. 44
   E. 50

43) A shirt costing $300 is discounted 15%. After a month, the shirt is discounted another 15%. Which of the following expressions can be used to find the selling price of the shirt?

   A. $(300)(0.70)$
   B. $(300) - 300\,(0.30)$
   C. $(300)(0.85)(0.85)$
   D. $(300)(0.15) - (300)(0.15)$
   E. $(300)(0.85)(0.85) - (300)(0.15)$

44) $6 + 8 \times (-2) - [4 + 22 \times 5] \div 6 = ?$

   A. 120
   B. 88
   C. -45
   D. -40
   E. -29

45) Four straight lines interest at point O as shown below. What is the value of x?

   A. $20°$
   B. $25°$
   C. $30°$
   D. $35°$
   E. $40°$

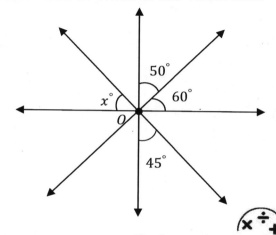

46) The table below shows the height of students. What is the average of height students?

A. 151
B. 157
C. 159
D. 161
E. 164

Students	Height
Alex	157
James	164
John	148
Lars	167
Nick	171
Edward	159

Questions 47 to 49 are based on the following data

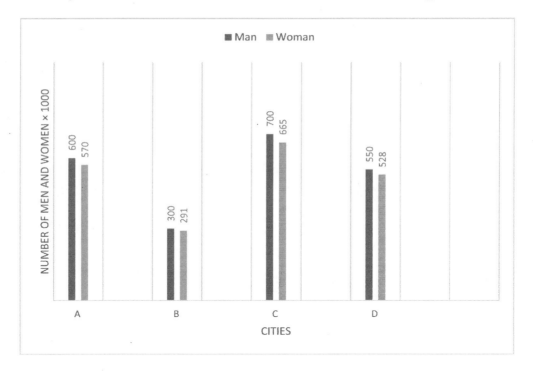

47) What's the maximum ratio of woman to man in the four cities?

A. 0.98
B. 0.97
C. 0.96
D. 0.95
E. 0.94

48) What's the ratio of percentage of men in city *A* to percentage of women in city *C*?

    A. 0.85

    B. 0.9

    C. 0.95

    D. 1

    E. 1.05

49) How many women should be added to city *D* until the ratio of women to men will be 1.2?

    A. 120

    B. 123

    C. 128

    D. 132

    E. 160

50) The circle graph below shows all Mr. Green's expenses for last month. If he spent $660 on his car, how much did he spend for his rent?

    A. $700

    B. $740

    C. $780

    D. $810

    E. $860

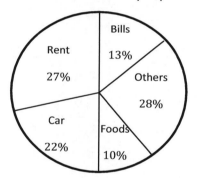

Mr. Green's monthly expenses

End of CBEST Mathematics Practice Test 1

CBEST Mathematics

Practice Test 2

2021–2022

Total number of questions: 50

Total time (Calculator): 90 Minutes

You may use a calculator on this practice test.

(On a real CBEST test, there is an onscreen calculator to use.)

15

Formula Sheet

Perimeter / Circumference

Rectangle

$Perimeter = 2(length) + 2(width)$

Circle

$Circumference = 2\pi(radius)$

Area

Circle

$Area = \pi(radius)^2$

Triangle

$Area = \frac{1}{2}(base)(height)$

Parallelogram

$Area = (base)(height)$

Trapezoid

$Area = \frac{1}{2}(base_1 + base_2)(height)$

Volume

Prism/Cylinder

$Volume = (area\ of\ the\ base)(height)$

Pyramid/Cone

$Volume = \frac{1}{3}(area\ of\ the\ base)(height)$

Sphere

$Volume = \frac{4}{3}\pi(radius)^3$

Length

1 foot = 12 inches

1 yard = 3 feet

1 mile = 5,280 feet

1 meter = 1,000 millimeters

1 meter = 100 centimeters

1 kilometer = 1,000 meters

1 mile ≈ 1.6 kilometers

1 inch = 2.54 centimeters

1 foot ≈ 0.3 meter

Capacity / Volume

1 cup = 8 fluid ounces

1 pint = 2 cups

1 quart = 2 pints

1 gallon = 4 quarts

1 gallon = 231 cubic inches

1 liter = 1,000 milliliters

1 liter ≈ 0.264 gallon

Weight

1 pound = 16 ounces

1 ton = 2,000 pounds

1 gram = 1,000 milligrams

1 kilogram = 1,000 grams

1 kilogram ≈ 2.2 pounds

1 ounce ≈ 28.3 grams

1) The mean of 50 test scores was calculated as 90. But it turned out that one of the scores was misread as 94 but it was 69. What is the mean?

   A. 25

   B. 85.2

   C. 87

   D. 89.5

   E. 90

2) Two dice are thrown simultaneously, what is the probability of getting a sum of 5 or 8?

   A. $\frac{1}{3}$

   B. $\frac{1}{4}$

   C. $\frac{1}{16}$

   D. $\frac{1}{36}$

   E. $\frac{11}{36}$

3) In the figure below, what is the value of x?

   A. 45°

   B. 67°

   C. 68°

   D. 135°

   E. 180°

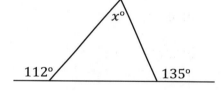

4) What is the value of the expression $6(x - 2y) + (2 - x)^2$ when $x = 3$ and $y = -2$?

   A. −5

   B. 5

   C. 41

   D. 43

   E. 67

5) A swimming pool holds 2,500 cubic feet of water. The swimming pool is 25 feet long and 10 feet wide. How deep is the swimming pool?

   A. 4 *feet*

   B. 6 *feet*

   C. 7 *feet*

   D. 10 *feet*

   E. 25 *feet*

6) Mr. Carlos family are choosing a menu for their reception. They have 2 choices of appetizers, 5 choices of entrees, 4 choices of cake. How many different menu combinations are possible for them to choose?

A. 12
B. 20
C. 32
D. 40
E. 60

7) Four one – foot rulers can be split among how many users to leave each with $\frac{1}{3}$ of a ruler?

A. 4
B. 6
C. 12
D. 24
E. 48

8) What is the area of a square whose diagonal is 4?

A. 4
B. 8
C. 16
D. 64
E. 124

9) In the following right triangle, if the sides AB and BC become twice longer, what will be the ratio of the perimeter of the triangle to its area?

A. $\frac{1}{2}$
B. $\frac{1}{5}$
C. $\frac{3}{2}$
D. 1
E. 2

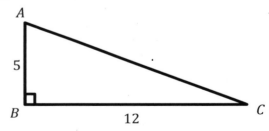

10) The average of five numbers is 26. If a sixth number 42 is added, then, what is the new average? (round your answer to the nearest hundredth).

A. 25
B. 26.5
C. 27
D. 28.67
E. 36

11) Mr. Jones saves $2,500 out of his monthly family income of $65,000. What fractional part of his income does he save?

A. $\frac{1}{11}$

B. $\frac{1}{15}$

C. $\frac{1}{26}$

D. $\frac{2}{15}$

E. $\frac{3}{25}$

12) A football team had $20,000 to spend on supplies. The team spent $14,000 on new balls. New sport shoes cost $110 each. Which of the following inequalities represent how many new shoes the team can purchase?

A. $110x + 14,000 \leq 20,000$

B. $110x + 14,000 \geq 20,000$

C. $14,000x + 110 \leq 20,000$

D. $14,000x + 110 \geq 20,000$

E. $14,000x + 14,000 \geq 20,000$

13) Jason needs an 70% average in his writing class to pass. On his first 4 exams, he earned scores of $68\%, 72\%, 85\%$, and 90%. What is the minimum score Jason can earn on his fifth and final test to pass?

A. 80%

B. 70%

C. 68%

D. 54%

E. 35%

14) A child grows $1\frac{1}{7}$ inches in $\frac{1}{5}$ of a year. What would be his yearly growth rate in inches per year?

A. $5\frac{7}{5}$

B. $5\frac{5}{7}$

C. $2\frac{1}{7}$

D. $1\frac{1}{12}$

E. $\frac{1}{12}$

15) A construction company is building a wall. The company can build 30 cm of the wall per minute. After 40 minutes $\frac{3}{4}$ of the wall is completed. How many meters is the wall?

   A. 4 m
   B. 12 m
   C. 16 m
   D. 30 m
   E. 40 m

16) Kim earned $55 an hour. John earned 10% less than Kim. How much money did John earn in an hour?

   A. $43.50
   B. $45.50
   C. $47.50
   D. $49.50
   E. $51.50

17) Last week 25,000 fans attended a football match. This week three times as many bought tickets, but one sixth of them cancelled their tickets. How many are attending this week?

   A. 48,000
   B. 54,000
   C. 62,500
   D. 75,000
   E. 84,000

18) What is the perimeter of a square that has an area of 49 square inches?

   A. 144 $inches$
   B. 64 $inches$
   C. 56 $inches$
   D. 48 $inches$
   E. 28 $inches$

19) If the area of the following rectangular $ABCD$ is 100, and E is the midpoint of AB, what is the area of the shaded part?

   A. 25
   B. 50
   C. 75
   D. 80
   E. 100

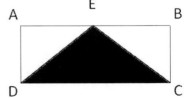

20) Set A contains all integers from 15 to 160, inclusive, and set B contains all integers from 74 to 180, inclusive. How many integers are included in A, but not in B?

    A. 56
    B. 57
    C. 58
    D. 59
    E. 60

21) If the ordered pair $(-4, 5)$ is reflected over the x-axis, what is the new ordered pair?

    A. $(4, 5)$
    B. $(-4, 5)$
    C. $(5, -4)$
    D. $(5, 4)$
    E. $(-4, -5)$

22) What is the ones digit in the divided of the problem below?

$$
\begin{array}{r}
12 \quad \text{Remainder} = 19 \\
23 \overline{)\,29\square}
\end{array}
$$

    A. 1
    B. 2
    C. 3
    D. 4
    E. 5

23) A taxi driver earns \$9 per 1−hour work. If he works 10 hours a day and in 1 hour he uses 2 −liters petrol with price \$1 for 1 −liter, how much money does he earn in one day?

    A. \$90
    B. \$88
    C. \$70
    D. \$60
    E. \$20

24) A cruise line ship left Port A and traveled 50 miles due east and then 120 miles due north. At this point, what is the shortest distance from the cruise to port A?

    A. 70 *miles*

    B. 80 *miles*

    C. 130 *miles*

    D. 150 *miles*

    E. 230 *miles*

25) What is the equivalent temperature of $104°F$ in Celsius?

$$C = \frac{5}{9}(F - 32)$$

    A. 32

    B. 40

    C. 48

    D. 52

    E. 64

26) Anita's trick–or–treat bag contains 15 pieces of chocolate, 10 suckers, 10 pieces of gum, 25 pieces of licorice. If she randomly pulls a piece of candy from her bag, what is the probability of her pulling out a piece of sucker?

    A. $\frac{1}{3}$

    B. $\frac{1}{4}$

    C. $\frac{1}{6}$

    D. $\frac{1}{12}$

    E. $\frac{1}{24}$

27) What is the missing term in the given sequence?

$$3, 4, 6, 9, 13, 18, 24, \underline{\quad}, 39$$

    A. 24

    B. 26

    C. 27

    D. 28

    E. 31

28) The perimeter of a rectangular yard is 72 meters. What is its length if its width is twice its length?

   A. 12 *meters*
   B. 18 *meters*
   C. 20 *meters*
   D. 24 *meters*
   E. 36 *meters*

29) How many positive integers satisfy the inequality $x + 5 < 21$?

   A. 10
   B. 12
   C. 14
   D. 15
   E. 17

30) What is the volume of a box with the following dimensions?
   High = 3 *cm*,   width = 5 *cm*,   length = 6 *cm*

   A. 15 cm^3
   B. 60 cm^3
   C. 90 cm^3
   D. 120 cm^3
   E. 240 cm^3

31) In two successive years, the population of a town is increased by 10% and 20%. What percent of the population is increased after two years?

   A. 30%
   B. 32%
   C. 35%
   D. 68%
   E. 70%

32) The sum of six different negative integers is -70. If the smallest of these integers is -15, what is the largest possible value of one of the other five integers?

   A. -15
   B. -14
   C. -10
   D. -5
   E. -1

33) If 20% of a number is 4, what is the number?

    A. 4

    B. 8

    C. 10

    D. 20

    E. 25

34) Jason left a $12.00 tip on a lunch that cost $40.00, approximately what percentage was the tip?

    A. 2.5%

    B. 10%

    C. 15%

    D. 20%

    E. 30%

35) Emily deposits 15% of $160 into a savings account, what is the amount of his deposit?

    A. $10

    B. $16

    C. $20

    D. $24

    E. $30

36) If A is 4 times of B and A is 12, what is the value of B?

    A. 2

    B. 3

    C. 4

    D. 5

    E. 6

37) Jason is 9 miles ahead of Joe running at 6.5 miles per hour and Joe is running at the speed of 8 miles per hour. How long does it take Joe to catch Jason?

    A. 3 *hours*

    B. 4 *hours*

    C. 6 *hours*

    D. 8 *hours*

    E. 10 *hours*

38) 44 students took an exam and 11 of them failed. What percent of the students passed the exam?

    A. 20%

    B. 40%

    C. 60%

    D. 75%

    E. 90%

39) In the following figure, MN is 40 *cm*. How long is ON?

    A. 25 *cm*

    B. 20 *cm*

    C. 15 *cm*

    D. 10 *cm*

    E. 5 *cm*

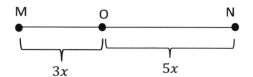

40) The diagonal of a rectangle is 10 inches long and the height of the rectangle is 6 inches. What is the perimeter of the rectangle?

    A. 10 *inches*

    B. 12 *inches*

    C. 16 *inches*

    D. 18 *inches*

    E. 28 *inches*

41) The cost, in thousands of dollars, of producing x thousands of textbooks is $C(x) = x^2 + 2x$. The revenue, also in thousands of dollars, is $R(x) = 40x$. Find the profit or loss if 30 textbooks are produced. (Profit = revenue − cost)

    A. $2,160 profit

    B. $2,160 loss

    C. $1,200 loss

    D. $240 profit

    E. $240 loss

42) If angle AOD measures 23°, what is the measure of angle DOC ?

    A. 23°

    B. 46°

    C. 67°

    D. 157°

    E. It cannot be determined from information given.

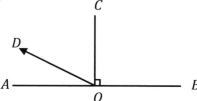

43) A card is drawn at random from a standard 52–card deck, what is the probability that the card is of Hearts? (The deck includes 13 of each suit clubs, diamonds, hearts, and spades)

A. $\frac{1}{2}$

B. $\frac{1}{4}$

C. $\frac{1}{6}$

D. $\frac{1}{52}$

E. $\frac{1}{104}$

44) Which of the following shows the numbers in descending order?

$$\frac{1}{3}, 0.68, 67\%, \frac{4}{5}$$

A. $67\%, 0.68, \frac{1}{3}, \frac{4}{5}$

B. $67\%, 0.68, \frac{4}{5}, \frac{1}{3}$

C. $0.68, 67\%, \frac{1}{3}, \frac{4}{5}$

D. $\frac{1}{3}, 67\%, 0.68, \frac{4}{5}$

E. $\frac{1}{3}, 67\%, \frac{4}{5}, 0.68$

45) Which of the following is the best estimate for $3,689 \times 340$?

A. 9,000,000

B. 1,200,000

C. 900,000

D. 120,000

E. 9,000

46) The table below shows a relationship between values of x and y. What is the value of y that is missing?

A. 4.75

B. 5.25

C. 5.5

D. 5.25

E. 5.75

x	y
2	3
2.5	3.75
3	4.5
3.5	...
4	6

47) What is the percent of cars is blue?

A. 18%
B. 20%
C. 23%
D. 26%
E. 33%

Cars of company

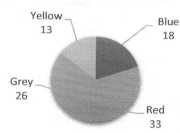

Use the table below to answer the question.

Students	Boys	Girls
Grade 5	24	16
Grade 6	18	27
Grade 7	14	19

48) The table above shows the number of students in a school. What percent of sixth grade students are girls?

A. 40%
B. 42%
C. 55%
D. 60%
E. 62%

Use the chart below to answer the question. The table below shows the number of different color marbles in a bag.

Color	Number of marbles
White	20
Black	30
Beige	40

49) There are also purple marbles in the bag. Which of the following can NOT be the probability of randomly selecting a purple marble from the bag?

A. $\frac{1}{10}$
B. $\frac{1}{4}$
C. $\frac{2}{5}$
D. $\frac{7}{15}$
E. $\frac{9}{15}$

Gender	Under 45	45 or older	total
Male	12	6	18
Female	5	7	12
Total	17	13	30

50) The table above shows the distribution of age and gender for 30 employees in a company. If one employee is selected at random, what is the probability that the employee selected be either a female under age 45 or a male age 45 or older?

A. $\frac{5}{6}$

B. $\frac{5}{30}$

C. $\frac{6}{30}$

D. $\frac{11}{30}$

E. $\frac{45}{30}$

End of CBEST Mathematics Practice Test 2

CBEST Mathematics

Practice Test 3

2021–2022

Total number of questions: 50

Total time (Calculator): 90 Minutes

You may use a calculator on this practice test.

(On a real CBEST test, there is an onscreen calculator to use.)

29

Formula Sheet

Perimeter / Circumference

Rectangle
Perimeter $= 2(length) + 2(width)$

Circle
Circumference $= 2\pi(radius)$

Area

Circle
Area $= \pi(radius)^2$

Triangle
Area $= \frac{1}{2}(base)(height)$

Parallelogram
Area $= (base)(height)$

Trapezoid
Area $= \frac{1}{2}(base_1 + base_2)(height)$

Volume

Prism/Cylinder
Volume $= (area\ of\ the\ base)(height)$

Pyramid/Cone
Volume $= \frac{1}{3}(area\ of\ the\ base)(height)$

Sphere
Volume $= \frac{4}{3}\pi(radius)^3$

Length

1 foot = 12 inches

1 yard = 3 feet

1 mile = 5,280 feet

1 meter = 1,000 millimeters

1 meter = 100 centimeters

1 kilometer = 1,000 meters

1 mile ≈ 1.6 kilometers

1 inch = 2.54 centimeters

1 foot ≈ 0.3 meter

Capacity / Volume

1 cup = 8 fluid ounces

1 pint = 2 cups

1 quart = 2 pints

1 gallon = 4 quarts

1 gallon = 231 cubic inches

1 liter = 1,000 milliliters

1 liter ≈ 0.264 gallon

Weight

1 pound = 16 ounces

1 ton = 2,000 pounds

1 gram = 1,000 milligrams

1 kilogram = 1,000 grams

1 kilogram ≈ 2.2 pounds

1 ounce ≈ 28.3 grams

1) If the area of the following trapezoid is $126\ cm$, what is the perimeter of the trapezoid? (Figure not drawn to scale.)

   A. 32
   B. 42
   C. 46
   D. 56
   E. 64

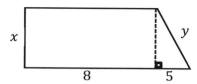

2) If 5 inches on a map represents an actual distance of 100 feet, then, what actual distance does 18 inches on the map represent?

   A. 18 feet
   B. 20 feet
   C. 100 feet
   D. 250 feet
   E. 360 feet

3) Which of the following lists shows the fractions in order from least to greatest?

$$\frac{3}{4}, \frac{2}{7}, \frac{3}{8}, \frac{5}{11}$$

   A. $\frac{3}{8}, \frac{2}{7}, \frac{3}{4}, \frac{5}{11}$
   B. $\frac{3}{8}, \frac{2}{7}, \frac{5}{11}, \frac{3}{4}$
   C. $\frac{2}{7}, \frac{5}{11}, \frac{3}{8}, \frac{3}{4}$
   D. $\frac{2}{7}, \frac{3}{8}, \frac{5}{11}, \frac{3}{4}$
   E. $\frac{5}{11}, \frac{3}{4}, \frac{3}{8}, \frac{2}{7}$

4) What is the value of 6^4?

   A. 6
   B. 24
   C. 36
   D. 216
   E. 1,296

5) How many $\frac{1}{5}$ pound paperback books together weigh 50 pounds?

   A. 25
   B. 50
   C. 150
   D. 200
   E. 250

6) What is the volume of the following square pyramid?

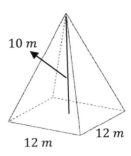

    A. $100 \ m^3$
    B. $120 \ m^3$
    C. $144 \ m^3$
    D. $480 \ m^3$
    E. $1,440 \ m^3$

7) What is the value of x in the following equation?

$$\frac{2}{3}x + \frac{1}{6} = \frac{1}{3}$$

    A. 6
    B. $\frac{1}{2}$
    C. $\frac{1}{3}$
    D. $\frac{1}{4}$
    E. $\frac{1}{12}$

8) In the following shape, the area of the circle is 16π. What is the area of the square?

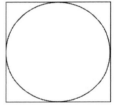

    A. 4
    B. 8
    C. 16
    D. 32
    E. 64

9) List A consists of the numbers $\{1, 3, 8, 10, 15\}$, and list B consists of the numbers $\{4, 6, 12, 14, 17\}$. If the two lists are combined, what is the median of the combined list?

    A. 9
    B. 10
    C. 12
    D. 15
    E. 17

10) What's the area of the non-shaded part of the following figure?

    A. 236
    B. 192
    C. 152
    D. 42
    E. 40

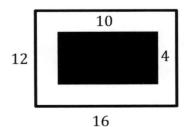

11) In the triangle below, if the measure of angle A is 37 degrees, then what is the value of y? (figure is NOT drawn to scale)

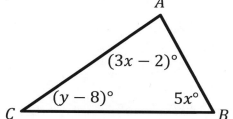

A. 37
B. 62
C. 70
D. 78
E. 86

12) There are only red and blue cards in a box. The probability of choosing a red card in the box at random is one third. If there are 246 blue cards, how many cards are in the box?

A. 123
B. 246
C. 308
D. 328
E. 369

13) In the diagram below, circle A represents the set of all odd numbers, circle B represents the set of all negative numbers, and circle C represents the set of all multiples of 5. Which number could be replaced with y?

A. 0
B. 5
C. −5
D. 10
E. −10

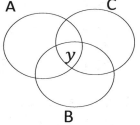

14) Which of the following is an obtuse angle?

A. 116°
B. 80°
C. 68°
D. 25°
E. 15°

15) A basket contains 20 balls and the average weight of each of these balls is 25 g. The five heaviest balls have an average weight of 40 g each. If we remove the five heaviest balls from the basket, what is the average weight of the remaining balls?

A. 10 g
B. 20 g
C. 30 g
D. 35 g
E. 40 g

16) In a stadium the ratio of home fans to visiting fans in a crowd is $5:7$. Which of the following could be the total number of fans in the stadium?

    A. 12,324
    B. 42,326
    C. 44,566
    D. 66,812
    E. 69,752

17) A bread recipe calls for $2\frac{2}{3}$ cups of flour. If you only have $1\frac{5}{6}$ cups, how much more flour is needed?

    A. 1
    B. 2
    C. $\frac{1}{2}$
    D. $\frac{5}{6}$
    E. $\frac{11}{6}$

18) If $x=\frac{1}{3}$ and $y=\frac{9}{21}$, then which is equal to $\frac{1}{x}\div\frac{y}{3}$?

    A. $\frac{1}{7}$
    B. $\frac{1}{3}$
    C. $\frac{2}{3}$
    D. $\frac{1}{21}$
    E. 21

19) Ella (E) is 4 years older than her friend Ava (A) who is 3 years younger than her sister Sofia (S). If E, A and S denote their ages, which one of the following represents the given information?

    A. $\begin{cases}E=A+4\\S=A-3\end{cases}$
    B. $\begin{cases}E=A+4\\A=S+3\end{cases}$
    C. $\begin{cases}A=E+4\\S=A-3\end{cases}$
    D. $\begin{cases}E=A+4\\A=S-3\end{cases}$
    E. $\begin{cases}E=A+3\\S=A+4\end{cases}$

20) If Jim adds 100 stamps to his current stamp collection, the total number of stamps will be equal to $\frac{6}{5}$ the current number of stamps. If Jim adds 50% more stamps to the current collection, how many stamps will be in the collection?

   A. 150
   B. 300
   C. 500
   D. 600
   E. 750

21) The sum of 8 numbers is greater than 240 and less than 320. Which of the following could be the average (arithmetic mean) of the numbers?

   A. 25
   B. 30
   C. 35
   D. 40
   E. 45

22) In the following figure, point Q lies on line n, what is the value of y if $x = 35$?

   A. 21
   B. 25
   C. 35
   D. 40
   E. 50

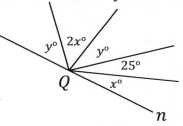

23) The length of a rectangle is 3 meters greater than 4 times its width. The perimeter of the rectangle is 36 meters. What is the area of the rectangle in meters?

   A. 15
   B. 35
   C. 45
   D. 55
   E. 65

24) What is the value of x?

   A. 38
   B. 45
   C. 75
   D. 83
   E. 135

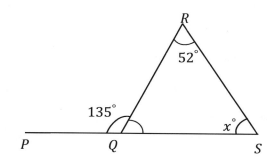

25) Find the value of x in the following diagram. (there are 2 supplementary angles in the diagram)

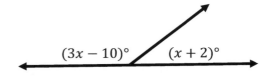

    A. 27

    B. 32

    C. 37

    D. 45

    E. 47

26) What is the area of the shaded region if the diameter of the bigger circle is 12 inches and the diameter of the smaller circle is 8 inches?

    A. $16\pi\ in^2$

    B. $20\pi\ in^2$

    C. $36\pi\ in^2$

    D. $48\pi\ in^2$

    E. $80\pi\ in^2$

27) Which of the following expressions is equivalent to $\dfrac{a+b}{2}$?

    A. $\dfrac{ab}{2}$

    B. $\dfrac{a}{2} \times \dfrac{b}{2}$

    C. $\dfrac{1}{2} \times a \times b$

    D. $\dfrac{a}{2} + \dfrac{b}{2}$

    E. $\dfrac{1}{2}(a \times b)$

28) What is 2.5% of 1,200?

    A. 900

    B. 600

    C. 300

    D. 60

    E. 30

29) If x is a real number, and if $x^3 + 18 = 130$, then x lies between which two consecutive integers?

    A. 1 and 2

    B. 2 and 3

    C. 3 and 4

    D. 4 and 5

    E. 5 and 6

30) Jack types 72 words per minute. How many words does he type in 15 seconds?

   A. 14

   B. 18

   C. 20

   D. 22

   E. 24

31) Jack earns $616 for his first 44 hours of work in a week and is then paid 1.5 times his regular hourly rate for any additional hours. This week, Jack needs $826 to pay his rent, bills and other expenses. How many hours must he work to make enough money in this week?

   A. 27

   B. 32

   C. 44

   D. 54

   E. 68

32) Which of the following is the same as: 0.000,000,000,000,042,121?

   A. 4.2121×10^{14}

   B. 4.2121×10^{13}

   C. 42.121×10^{-10}

   D. 42.121×10^{-13}

   E. 4.2121×10^{-14}

33) Which of the following is the largest?

   A. $|4 - 2|$

   B. $|2 - 4|$

   C. $|-2 - 4|$

   D. $|2 - 4| - |4 - 2|$

   E. $|2 - 4| + |4 - 2|$

34) A student gets 85% of a test with 40 questions. How many answers did the student solve correctly?

   A. 15

   B. 24

   C. 26

   D. 34

   E. 36

35) To buy a new computer, Emma borrowed $2,500 at 8% interest for 6 years. How much interest did she pay?

   A. $150

   B. $1,200

   C. $1,500

   D. $2,400

   E. $2,500

36) Integer x is evenly divisible by 4. Which expression below is also evenly divisible by 4?

   A. $x + 1$
   B. $2x + 1$
   C. $2x + 4$
   D. $3x + 2$
   E. $4x + 1$

Use the figure below to answer the question.

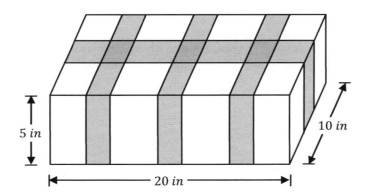

37) Ribbon is wrapped around the box, if 10% is added to the length of the ribbon for the bow tie, what is the length of the ribbon?

   A. 100 *in*
   B. 110 *in*
   C. 140 *in*
   D. 150 *in*
   E. 154 *in*

38) Sara has a box containing 5 blue balls, 8 red balls, and 3 green balls. If she removes one ball at random, what is the probability that it will not be blue?

    A. $\frac{1}{8}$

    B. $\frac{5}{16}$

    C. $\frac{5}{11}$

    D. $\frac{10}{11}$

    E. $\frac{11}{16}$

39) Jack rides 160 kilometers in 1 hour 20 minutes. At that rate, how many meters does he ride per minute?

    A. 1,000 meters

    B. 1,500 meters

    C. 1,600 meters

    D. 2,000 meters

    E. 2,500 meters

40) The sum of two consecutive integer is -13. If 2 is added to the smaller integer and 3 is subtract from the larger integer, what is the product of the two resulting integers?

    A. 5

    B. 9

    C. 18

    D. 28

    E. 45

41) If n is an even integer that is less than -3.34, what is the greatest possible value of n?

    A. -1

    B. -2

    C. -3

    D. -4

    E. -5

42) Find the value of x? $(2)^3 + (-3)^2 + 2x - 6 = 11$

    A. 0

    B. 2

    C. 4

    D. 6

    E. 8

43) A ladder leans against a wall forming a 60° angle between the ground and the ladder. If the bottom of the ladder is 30 feet away from the wall, how long is the ladder?

    A. 30 feet

    B. 40 feet

    C. 50 feet

    D. 60 feet

    E. 120 feet

Use the figure below answer the question.

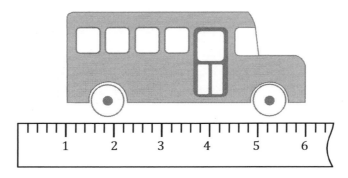

44) In the scale of the diagram is 1 unit = 160 centimeters, what is the actual size of the bus?

    A. 80 centimeters

    B. 800 centimers

    C. 96 centimeters

    D. 960 centimeters

    E. 9,600 centimeters

45) The table below displays a relationship between values of x and y. Which of the following expressions describe this relationship?

    A. $y = \frac{2}{3}x$

    B. $y = \frac{3}{2}x$

    C. $y = 2(x - 1)$

    D. $y = 3x - 1$

    E. $y = 4x - 2$

x	y
2	5
4	11
6	17
8	23
10	29

Questions 46 to 48 are based on the following data

Types of air pollutions in 10 cities of a country

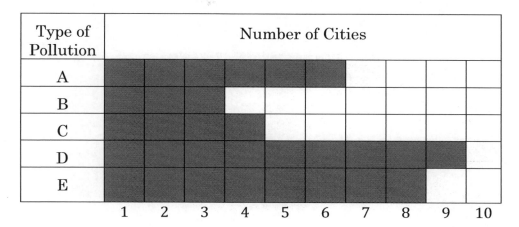

Type of Pollution	Number of Cities									
A										
B										
C										
D										
E										
	1	2	3	4	5	6	7	8	9	10

46) If a is the mean (average) of the number of cities in each pollution type category, b is the mode, and c is the median of the number of cities in each pollution type category, then which of the following must be true?

    A. $a < b < c$

    B. $b < a < c$

    C. $b < c < b$

    D. $a = c$

    E. $b < c = a$

47) What percent of cities are in the type of pollution A, C, and D respectively?

    A. 60%, 40%, 90%

    B. 40%, 90%, 60%

    C. 40%, 60%, 90%

    D. 30%, 40%, 90%

    E. 30%, 40%, 60%

48) How many cities should be added to type of pollutions B until the ratio of cities in type of pollution B to cities in type of pollution E will be 0.625?

    A. 2

    B. 3

    C. 4

    D. 5

    E. 6

Use the table below to answer the question.

Appliances	Price
Sofa	$365.76
Washing machine	$289.55
Oven	$378.45
TV	$289.99
Refrigerators	$1,459
Dishwasher	?

49) Emily has bought appliances for her new home. The total cost of her purchase is $3,332.49. What is the missing price?

A. $450.74

B. $549.47

C. $549.74

D. $640.64

E. $748.74

50) The following graph shows the mark of seven students in mathematics. What is the mean (average) of the marks?

A. 15

B. 14.5

C. 14

D. 13.5

E. 13

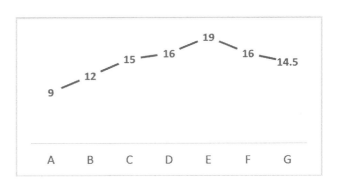

End of CBEST Mathematics Practice Test 3

CBEST Mathematics

Practice Test 4

2021–2022

Total number of questions: 50

Total time (Calculator): 90 Minutes

You may use a calculator on this practice test.

(On a real CBEST test, there is an onscreen calculator to use.)

43

Formula Sheet

Perimeter / Circumference

Rectangle

$Perimeter = 2(length) + 2(width)$

Circle

$Circumference = 2\pi(radius)$

Area

Circle

$Area = \pi(radius)^2$

Triangle

$Area = \frac{1}{2}(base)(height)$

Parallelogram

$Area = (base)(height)$

Trapezoid

$Area = \frac{1}{2}(base_1 + base_2)(height)$

Volume

Prism/Cylinder

$Volume = (area\ of\ the\ base)(height)$

Pyramid/Cone

$Volume = \frac{1}{3}(area\ of\ the\ base)(height)$

Sphere

$Volume = \frac{4}{3}\pi(radius)^3$

Length

1 foot = 12 inches

1 yard = 3 feet

1 mile = 5,280 feet

1 meter = 1,000 millimeters

1 meter = 100 centimeters

1 kilometer = 1,000 meters

1 mile ≈ 1.6 kilometers

1 inch = 2.54 centimeters

1 foot ≈ 0.3 meter

Capacity / Volume

1 cup = 8 fluid ounces

1 pint = 2 cups

1 quart = 2 pints

1 gallon = 4 quarts

1 gallon = 231 cubic inches

1 liter = 1,000 milliliters

1 liter ≈ 0.264 gallon

Weight

1 pound = 16 ounces

1 ton = 2,000 pounds

1 gram = 1,000 milligrams

1 kilogram = 1,000 grams

1 kilogram ≈ 2.2 pounds

1 ounce ≈ 28.3 grams

1) The capacity of a red box is 20% bigger than the capacity of a blue box. If the red box can hold 30 equal sized books, how many of the same books can the blue box hold?

   A. 9
   B. 15
   C. 21
   D. 25
   E. 30

2) Kim spent $35 for pants. This was $10 less than triple what she spent for a shirt. How much was the shirt?

   A. $11
   B. $13
   C. $15
   D. $17
   E. $21

3) What is the greatest integer less than $-\frac{32}{5}$?

   A. 0
   B. −2
   C. −4
   D. −6
   E. −7

4) The measure of the angles of a triangle are in the ratio $1: 3: 5$. What is the measure of the largest angle?

   A. $20°$
   B. $45°$
   C. $85°$
   D. $100°$
   E. $180°$

5) In the figure below, line A is parallel to line B. what is the value of x?

   A. 28
   B. 46
   C. 50
   D. 55
   E. 65

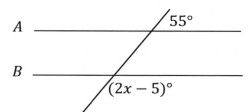

6) In the infinitely repeating decimal below, 1 is the first digit in the repeating pattern. What is the $68th$ digit? $\frac{1}{7} = 0.\overline{142857}$

  A. 1

  B. 2

  C. 4

  D. 5

  E. 7

7) In the following figure, $ABCD$ is a rectangle. If $a = \sqrt{3}$, and $b = 2a$, find the area of the shaded region. (the shaded region is a trapezoid)

  A. $2\sqrt{3}$

  B. $3\sqrt{3}$

  C. $4\sqrt{3}$

  D. $6\sqrt{3}$

  E. $8\sqrt{3}$

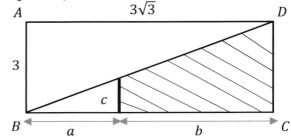

8) The supplement angle of a 45° angle is:

  A. 135°

  B. 105°

  C. 90°

  D. 35°

  E. 15°

9) Anna opened an account with a deposit of $3,000. This account earns 5% simple interest annually. How many years will it take her to earn $600 on her $3,000 deposit?

  A. 2

  B. 4

  C. 5

  D. 6

  E. 8

10) A list of consecutive integers begins with k and ends with n. If $n - k = 46$, how many integers are in the list?

  A. 23

  B. 38

  C. 46

  D. 47

  E. 58

11) Tom picked $2\frac{2}{5}$ baskets of apples, and Sam picked $1\frac{3}{4}$ baskets of apples. How many baskets total did they pick?

    A. $1\frac{2}{3}$

    B. $2\frac{1}{12}$

    C. $3\frac{20}{23}$

    D. $4\frac{3}{20}$

    E. $5\frac{1}{12}$

12) A piece of paper that is $2\frac{3}{5}$ feet long is cut into 2 pieces of different lengths. The shorter piece has a length of x feet. Which inequality expresses all possible values of x?

    A. $x < 2\frac{1}{10}$

    B. $x > 2$

    C. $x < 2\frac{3}{5}$

    D. $x > 1\frac{3}{10}$

    E. $x < 1\frac{3}{10}$

13) In an academy, course grades range from 0 to 100. Anna took 5 courses and her mean course grade was 80. William took 8 courses. If both students have the same sum of course grades, what was William's mean?

    A. 50

    B. 65

    C. 70

    D. 80

    E. 85

14) The set S consists of all odd numbers greater than 5 and less than 30. What is the mean of the numbers in S?

    A. 11

    B. 13

    C. 17

    D. 18

    E. 23

15) In a group of 45 student, 60% can't swim. How many students can swim?

    A. 13

    B. 18

    C. 22

    D. 23

    E. 35

16) $8,400 are distributed equally among 14 person. How much money will each person get?

    A. $400

    B. $450

    C. $584

    D. $600

    E. $800

17) A box contains 6 green sticks, 4 blue sticks, and 2 yellow sticks. Emma picks one without looking. What is the probability that the stick will be green?

    A. $\frac{1}{2}$

    B. $\frac{1}{3}$

    C. $\frac{1}{4}$

    D. $\frac{2}{5}$

    E. $\frac{3}{2}$

18) The price of a Chocolate was raised from $5.40 to $5.67. What was the percent increase in the price?

    A. 4%

    B. 5%

    C. 6%

    D. 8%

    E. 10%

19) In a box of blue and black marbles, the ratio of blue marbles to black marbles is 4: 3. If the box contains 150 black marbles, how many blue marbles are there?

    A. 100

    B. 150

    C. 200

    D. 300

    E. 600

20) $\frac{5}{8}$ of a number is 90. Find the number.

    A. 144

    B. 270

    C. 450

    D. 720

    E. 800

21) A juice mixture contains $\frac{5}{14}$ jar of cherry juice and $\frac{5}{70}$ jar of apple juice. How many jars of cherry juice per jar of apple juice does the mixture contain?

    A. 70

    B. 14

    C. 10

    D. 7

    E. 5

22) The set of possible values of n is $\{5, 3, 7\}$. What is the set of possible values of m if $2m = n + 5$?

    A. $\{2, 4, 7\}$

    B. $\{3, 2, 5\}$

    C. $\{4, 5, 8\}$

    D. $\{5, 4, 6\}$

    E. $\{6, 5, 8\}$

23) If $x = 25$, then which of the following equations are correct?

    A. $x + 10 = 40$

    B. $4x = 100$

    C. $3x = 70$

    D. $\frac{x}{2} = 12$

    E. $\frac{x}{3} = 8$

24) Jack scored a mean of 80 per test in his first 4 tests. In his 5th test, he scored 90. What was Jack's mean score for the 5 tests?

    A. 70

    B. 75

    C. 80

    D. 82

    E. 93

25) The volume of a cube is less than $64\ m^3$. Which of the following can be the cube's side?

   A. $2\ m$

   B. $4\ m$

   C. $8\ m$

   D. $10\ m$

   E. $11\ m$

26) What is the area of an isosceles right triangle that has one leg that measures $6\ cm$?

   A. $16\ cm^2$

   B. $18\ cm^2$

   C. $24\ cm^2$

   D. $32\ cm^2$

   E. $36\ cm^2$

27) If $0.00104 = \frac{104}{x}$, what is the value of x?

   A. $1,000$

   B. $10,000$

   C. $100,000$

   D. $1,000,000$

   E. $10,000,000$

28) A bag is filled with numbered cards from 1 to 15 and picked on at random. What is the probability that the card picked is number 8?

   A. $\frac{8}{15}$

   B. $\frac{7}{15}$

   C. $\frac{5}{15}$

   D. $\frac{2}{15}$

   E. $\frac{1}{15}$

29) What is the value of x in the figure below?

   A. 21

   B. 26

   C. 36

   D. 46

   E. 48

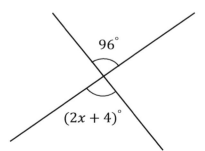

30) How many different two-digit numbers can be formed from the digits 6, 7, and 5, if the numbers must be even and no digit can be repeated?

   A. 1
   B. 2
   C. 3
   D. 4
   E. 5

31) A rectangular concrete driveway is 25 feet long, 6 feet wide, and 24 inches thick. What is the volume of the concrete?

   A. $300\ ft^3$
   B. $600\ ft^3$
   C. $660\ ft^3$
   D. $963\ ft^3$
   E. $1,800\ ft^3$

32) $200(3 + 0.01)^2 - 200 =$

   A. 201.55
   B. 361.08
   C. 702.88
   D. 1,612.02
   E. 1,812.02

33) If $360\ kg$ of vegetables is packed in 90 boxes, how much vegetables will each box contain?

   A. $2.5\ kg$
   B. $3\ kg$
   C. $4\ kg$
   D. $6.5\ kg$
   E. $7\ kg$

34) Each number in a sequence is 4 more than twice the number that comes just before it. If 84 is a number in the sequence, what number comes just before it?

   A. 26
   B. 35
   C. 40
   D. 52
   E. 88

35) $[6 \times (-24) + 8] - (-4) + [4 \times 5] \div 2 = ?$

    A. 148

    B. 132

    C. −122

    D. −136

    E. −144

36) A rectangle has $14\,cm$ wide and $5\,cm$ length. What is the perimeter of this rectangle?

    A. $19\,cm$

    B. $28\,cm$

    C. $33\,cm$

    D. $38\,cm$

    E. $41\,cm$

37) What is the value of the following expression? $3\frac{1}{4} + 2\frac{4}{16} + 1\frac{3}{8} + 5\frac{1}{2}$

    A. $3\frac{10}{14}$

    B. $4\frac{1}{2}$

    C. $12\frac{4}{16}$

    D. $12\frac{3}{8}$

    E. $12\frac{4}{8}$

38) A certain insect has a mass of 85 milligrams. What is the insect's mass in grams?

    A. 0.085

    B. 0.08

    C. 0.85

    D. 8.5

    E. 85

39) Removing which of the following numbers will change the average of the numbers to 6?

$$1, 4, 5, 8, 11, 12$$

    A. 1

    B. 4

    C. 5

    D. 8

    E. 11

40) If $m = 6$ and $n = -3$, what is the value of $\frac{5-9(3+n)}{3m-5(2-n)} = ?$

    A. $\frac{2}{7}$

    B. $\frac{3}{7}$

    C. $-\frac{4}{7}$

    D. $\frac{5}{7}$

    E. $-\frac{5}{7}$

41) Clara has 28 cookies. She is inviting 7 friends to a party. How many cookies will each friend get?

    A. 2

    B. 4

    C. 7

    D. 8

    E. 21

42) How long will it take to receive $360 in investment of $240 at the rate of 10% simple interest?

    A. 9 years

    B. 15 years

    C. 18 years

    D. 21 years

    E. 24 years

43) How many hours are there in 1,800 minutes?

    A. 20 hours

    B. 25 hours

    C. 30 hours

    D. 33 hours

    E. 60 hours

44) What is the value of x in the following equation? $|34 - 78| - x + |-12 + 20| = 36$

    A. 0

    B. 16

    C. 23

    D. 33

    E. 72

45) Mr. Alex wants to fence around a part of his land: (shown below), what is the total length of the fence?

A. 54

B. 56

C. 58

D. 60

E. 62

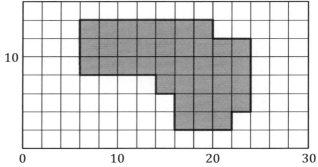

46) According to the following graph, how many more cars did John's sell in 2015 than in 2013

A. 100

B. 200

C. 250

D. 300

D. 400

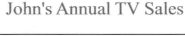

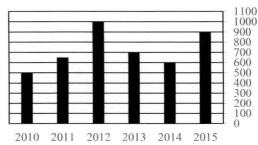

The table below shows the population of a village over five years.

Village	population
1993	1,153
1994	1,434
1995	1,850
1996	2,183
1997	2,923

47) What is the percent increase in population in 1996 compared to 1995?

A. 8%

B. 12%

C. 15%

D. 18%

E. 25%

Use the information below to answer the question.

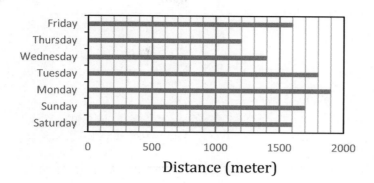

48) The diagram above shows the distance that John run during the week. What is his average distance during the week?

A. 1,300
B. 1,400
C. 1,500
D. 1,600
E. 1,700

Questions 49 to 50 are based on the following data

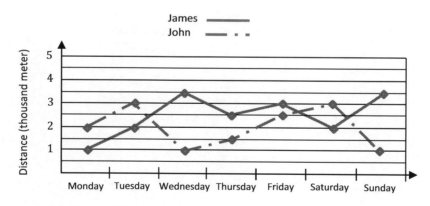

49) The chart above shows the distance James and John run in a week. First, find the average amount of James and John running in a week. What is the difference between the two average values?

A. 500 meters
B. 1,000 meters
C. 1,500 meters
D. 2,000 meters
E. 2,500 meters

50) What is the difference between the maximum and minimum distance of James running in a week?

A. 500 meters

B. 1,500 meters

C. 1,000 meters

D. 2,000 meters

E. 2,500 meters

End of CBEST Mathematics Practice Test 4

CBEST Mathematics

Practice Test 5

2021–2022

Total number of questions: 50

Total time (Calculator): 90 Minutes

You may use a calculator on this practice test.

(On a real CBEST test, there is an onscreen calculator to use.)

57

Formula Sheet

Perimeter / Circumference

Rectangle

$Perimeter = 2(length) + 2(width)$

Circle

$Circumference = 2\pi(radius)$

Area

Circle

$Area = \pi(radius)^2$

Triangle

$Area = \frac{1}{2}(base)(height)$

Parallelogram

$Area = (base)(height)$

Trapezoid

$Area = \frac{1}{2}(base_1 + base_2)(height)$

Volume

Prism/Cylinder

$Volume = (area\ of\ the\ base)(height)$

Pyramid/Cone

$Volume = \frac{1}{3}(area\ of\ the\ base)(height)$

Sphere

$Volume = \frac{4}{3}\pi(radius)^3$

Length

1 foot = 12 inches

1 yard = 3 feet

1 mile = 5,280 feet

1 meter = 1,000 millimeters

1 meter = 100 centimeters

1 kilometer = 1,000 meters

1 mile ≈ 1.6 kilometers

1 inch = 2.54 centimeters

1 foot ≈ 0.3 meter

Capacity / Volume

1 cup = 8 fluid ounces

1 pint = 2 cups

1 quart = 2 pints

1 gallon = 4 quarts

1 gallon = 231 cubic inches

1 liter = 1,000 milliliters

1 liter ≈ 0.264 gallon

Weight

1 pound = 16 ounces

1 ton = 2,000 pounds

1 gram = 1,000 milligrams

1 kilogram = 1,000 grams

1 kilogram ≈ 2.2 pounds

1 ounce ≈ 28.3 grams

1) A shoe originally priced at $45.00 was on sale for 15% off. Nick received a 20% employee discount applied to the sale price. How much did Nick pay for the shoes?

   A. $30.60
   B. $34.50
   C. $37.30
   D. $38.25
   E. $42.25

2) Which of the following values when entered in the box will satisfy the statement below?

$$\frac{5}{8} < \square < \frac{4}{5}$$

   A. $\frac{2}{5}$
   B. $\frac{3}{4}$
   C. $\frac{6}{10}$
   D. $\frac{3}{5}$
   E. $\frac{7}{8}$

3) What is the probability a D on of spinning the spinner?

   A. $\frac{1}{5}$
   B. $\frac{1}{10}$
   C. $\frac{3}{10}$
   D. $\frac{2}{5}$
   E. $\frac{3}{10}$

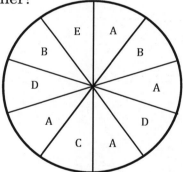

4) Which of the following is a factor of 45?

   A. 7
   B. 9
   C. 11
   D. 13
   E. 14

5) By what percent did the price of a shirt increase if its price was increased from $15.30 to $18.36?

     A. 10%

     B. 12%

     C. 16%

     D. 20%

     E. 22%

6) The greatest common factor of 32 and x is 8. How many possible values for x are greater than 10 and less than 60?

     A. 1

     B. 4

     C. 6

     D. 7

     E. 9

7) A box contains 6 strawberry candies, 4 orange candies, and 3 banana candies. If Roberto selects 2 candies at random from this box, without replacement, what is the probability that both candies are not orange?

     A. $\frac{1}{28}$

     B. $\frac{2}{13}$

     C. $\frac{6}{13}$

     D. $\frac{1}{3}$

     E. $\frac{2}{3}$

8) How many integers are between $\frac{7}{2}$ and $\frac{30}{4}$?

     A. 3

     B. 4

     C. 6

     D. 10

     E. 12

9) In a certain state, the sales tax rate increased from 8% to 8.5%. What was the increase in the sales tax on a $250 item?

     A. $0.5

     B. $1.00

     C. $1.25

     D. $1.90

     E. $2.30

10) Triangle ABC is graphed on a coordinate grid with vertices at $A(-3,-2)$, $B(-1,4)$ and $C(7,9)$. Triangle ABC is reflected over x axes to create triangle $A'B'C'$. Which order pair represents the coordinate of C'?

     A. $(-7,-9)$
     B. $(-7,9)$
     C. $(7,-9)$
     D. $(7,9)$
     E. $(9,7)$

11) Made a list of all possible products of 2 different numbers in the set below. What fraction of the products are odd?

$$\{1,4,6,5,7\}$$

     A. $\dfrac{2}{5}$
     B. $\dfrac{3}{10}$
     C. $\dfrac{7}{10}$
     D. $\dfrac{4}{15}$
     E. $\dfrac{8}{17}$

12) If $5n$ is a positive even number, how many odd numbers are in the range from $5n$ up to and including $5n + 6$?

     A. 1
     B. 2
     C. 3
     D. 4
     E. 5

13) If the actual Height of the building is 2,760 centimeters, then what is the scale of the diagram of the building?

     A. $1\ unit = 552\ centimeter$
     B. $1\ unit = 650\ centimeter$
     C. $1\ unit = 680\ centimeter$
     D. $1\ unit = 690\ centimeter$
     E. $1\ unit = 700\ centimeter$

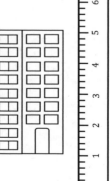

14) If $b = 2$ and $\frac{a}{4} = b$, what is the value of $a^2 + 4b$?

   A. 54

   B. 66

   C. 72

   D. 76

   E. 81

15) Which percentage is closest in value to 0.0099?

   A. 0.1%

   B. 1%

   C. 2%

   D. 9%

   E. 100%

16) What is the surface area of the cylinder below?

   A. $48\pi\ in^2$

   B. $57\pi\ in^2$

   C. $66\pi\ in^2$

   D. $288\pi\ in^2$

   E. $400\pi\ in^2$

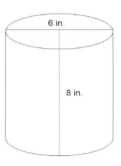

17) A train travels 1,500 miles from New York to Oklahoma. The train covers the first 280 miles in 4 hours. If the train continues to travel at this rate, how many more hours will it take to reach Oklahoma City? Round your answer to the nearest whole hour.

   A. 12

   B. 15

   C. 17

   D. 20

   E. 22

18) The sales price of a laptop is $1,912.50, which is 15% off the original price. What is the original price of the laptop?

   A. $2,750

   B. $2,250

   C. $1,625.625

   D. $956.25

   E. $286.875

19) In a scale diagram, 0.15 inch represents 150 feet. How many inches represent 2.5 *feet*?

    A. 0.001 *in*

    B. 0.002 *in*

    C. 0.0025 *in*

    D. 0.01 *in*

    E. 0.012 *in*

20) If $\frac{3}{7}$ of Z is 54, what is $\frac{2}{5}$ of Z?

    A. 44.2

    B. 46.3

    C. 48.4

    D. 50.4

    E. 60.6

21) A car travels at a speed of 72 miles per hour. How far will it travel in 8 hours?

    A. 576

    B. 540

    C. 480

    D. 432

    E. 272

22) If Sam spent $60 on sweets and he spent 25% of the selling price for the tip, how much did he spend?

    A. $66

    B. $69

    C. $72

    D. $75

    E. $77

23) Which of the following numbers has factors that include the smallest factor (other than 1) of 95?

    A. 25

    B. 28

    C. 32

    D. 39

    E. 45

24) $\dfrac{4^2+3^2+(-5)^2}{(9+10-11)^2} = ?$

   A. $\dfrac{25}{32}$

   B. $-\dfrac{25}{32}$

   C. 56

   D. -56

   E. 64

25) Angle A and angle B are supplementary. The measure of angle A is 2 times the measure of angle B. What is the measure of angle A in degrees?

   A. 100°

   B. 120°

   C. 140°

   D. 160°

   E. 170°

26) Tomas is 6 feet 8.5 inches tall, and Alex is 5 feet 3 inches tall. What is the difference in height, in inches, between Alex and Tomas?

   A. 2.5

   B. 7.5

   C. 12.5

   D. 17.5

   E. 19.5

27) Yesterday Kylie writes 10% of her homework. Today she writes another 18% of the entire homework. What fraction of the homework is left for her to write?

   A. $\dfrac{4}{25}$

   B. $\dfrac{7}{25}$

   C. $\dfrac{10}{25}$

   D. $\dfrac{18}{25}$

   E. $\dfrac{21}{25}$

28) In a box of blue and yellow pens, the ratio of yellow pens to blue pens is $2:3$. If the box contains 9 blue pens, how many yellow pens are there?

   A. 2

   B. 3

   C. 4

   D. 5

   E. 6

29) What decimal is equivalent to $-\frac{6}{9}$?

   A. $-0.\overline{5}$
   B. $-0.\overline{6}$
   C. $-0.\overline{65}$
   D. $-0.\overline{7}$
   E. $-0.\overline{75}$

30) The area of a circle is 81π. What is the diameter of the circle?

   A. 3
   B. 6
   C. 8
   D. 9
   E. 18

31) Five years ago, Amy was three times as old as Mike was. If Mike is 10 years old now, how old is Amy?

   A. 4
   B. 8
   C. 12
   D. 14
   E. 20

32) How many positive even factors of 68 are greater than 26 and less than 60?

   A. 0
   B. 1
   C. 2
   D. 4
   E. 6

33) The ratio of two sides of a parallelogram is $2:3$. If its perimeter is $40\ cm$, find the length of its sides.

   A. $6\ cm, 12\ cm$
   B. $8\ cm, 12\ cm$
   C. $10\ cm, 14\ cm$
   D. $12\ cm, 16\ cm$
   E. $14\ cm, 18\ cm$

34) What is the value of x in the following equation? $\frac{3}{4}(x-2) = 3\left(\frac{1}{6}x - \frac{3}{2}\right)$

   A. $\frac{1}{4}$

   B. $-\frac{3}{4}$

   C. -3

   D. 6

   E. -12

35) If x can be any integer, what is the greatest possible value of the expression $2 - x^2$?

   A. -1

   B. 0

   C. 2

   D. 3

   E. 4

36) A store has a container of handballs: 6 green, 5 blue, 8 white, and 10 yellow. If one ball is picked from the container at random, what is the probability that it will be green?

   A. $\frac{1}{5}$

   B. $\frac{6}{11}$

   C. $\frac{6}{29}$

   D. $\frac{8}{25}$

   E. $\frac{11}{25}$

37) Emma answered 9 out of 45 questions on a test incorrectly. What percentage of the questions did she answer correctly?

   A. 10%

   B. 40%

   C. 68%

   D. 80%

   E. 92%

38) If 30% of a number is 12, what is the number?

   A. 12

   B. 25

   C. 40

   D. 45

   E. 50

39) If Anna multiplies her age by 5 and then adds 3, she will get a number equal to her mother's age. If x is her mother's age, what is Anna's age in terms of x?

A. $\dfrac{x-3}{5}$

B. $\dfrac{x-5}{3}$

C. $3x + 5$

D. $5x - 3$

E. $x - 3$

40) A line connects the midpoint of AB (point E), with point C in the square $ABCD$. Calculate the area of the acquired trapezoid shape if the square has a side of $4\ m$.

A. $4\ cm^2$

B. $12\ cm^2$

C. $15\ cm^2$

D. $18\ cm^2$

E. $24\ cm^2$

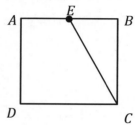

41) Which of the following is between 0.0048 and 0.069 ?

A. 0.07

B. 0.0039

C. 0.091

D. 0.081

E. 0.061

42) The reciprocal of $\dfrac{3}{5}$ is added to the reciprocal of $\dfrac{1}{4}$. What is the reciprocal of this sum?

A. $\dfrac{3}{5}$

B. $\dfrac{5}{3}$

C. $\dfrac{3}{17}$

D. $\dfrac{17}{3}$

E. $\dfrac{19}{3}$

43) What is the solution to $\dfrac{0.02}{0.25} = \dfrac{1.25}{x}$?

A. 0.150

B. 1.156

C. 11.565

D. 15.625

E. 16.625

44) Which of the following numbers is greater than −0.0029 ?

    A. −0.003

    B. −0.029

    C. −0.03

    D. −0.0028

    E. −0.028

45) The weight of a pan is 3 pounds and 8 ounces. What is the weight of 5 pan?

    A. 16 pounds and 6 ounces

    B. 16 pounds and 8 ounces

    C. 17 pounds and 6 ounces

    D. 17 pounds and 8 ounces

    E. 18 pounds and 8 ounces

Use the graph below to answer the question.

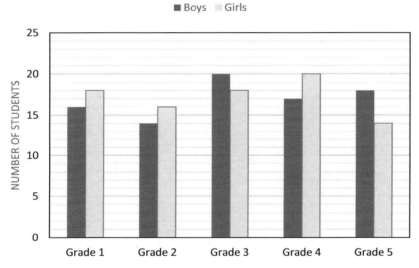

46) According to the chart above, which class has the least number of girl students?

    A. Grade 1

    B. Grade 2

    C. Grade 3

    D. Grade 4

    E. Grade 5

Use the chart below to answer the question.

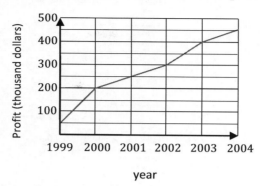

47) What is the percent increase for profit from 2001 to 2003?

A. 60%

B. 55%

C. 44%

D. 40%

E. 20%

Use the graph below to answer the question.

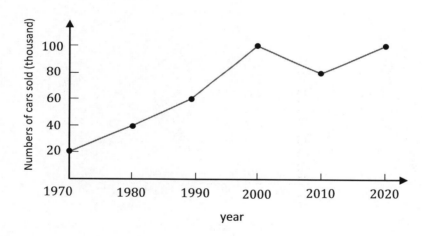

48) The graph shows the number of cars sold by a company over 50 years. Between what years did the number of sales increase by the greatest amount?

A. Between 1970 and 1980

B. Between 1980 and 1990

C. Between 1990 and 2000

D. Between 2000 and 2010

E. Between 2010 and 2020

Use the table below to answer the question.

Fruit name	harvest
Orange	200 thousand
Apple	500 thousand
Watermelon	250 thousand
Banana	150 thousand

49) The table above shows Mr. Sullivan's garden harvest. According to the table, what was his total harvest?

A. 1,100
B. 11,000
C. 110,000
D. 1,100,000
E. 11,000,000

Use the graphs below to answer the question.

Produced by a car factory

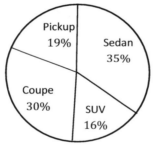

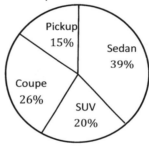

Revenue from sales in 2000   Revenue from sales in 2006
$850,000 $980,000

50) What is the difference between the amount of revenue earned from the sale of SUVs in 2006 compared to 2000?

A. 1,000
B. 3,000
C. 6,000
D. 30,000
E. 60,000

End of CBEST Mathematics Practice Test 5

CBEST Mathematics Practice Tests Answer Keys

Now, it's time to review your results to see where you went wrong and what areas you need to improve.

	CBEST Practice Test 1						CBEST Practice Test 2					
1	C	21	E	41	D	1	D	21	E	41	D
2	C	22	B	42	A	2	B	22	E	42	C
3	D	23	A	43	C	3	B	23	C	43	B
4	C	24	E	44	E	4	D	24	C	44	D
5	D	25	C	45	B	5	D	25	B	45	B
6	E	26	C	46	D	6	D	26	C	46	D
7	E	27	D	47	B	7	C	27	E	47	B
8	D	28	C	48	E	8	B	28	A	48	D
9	C	29	E	49	D	9	A	29	D	49	D
10	E	30	D	50	D	10	D	30	C	50	D
11	C	31	A			11	C	31	B	
12	C	32	D			12	A	32	D	
13	B	33	C			13	E	33	D	
14	E	34	B			14	B	34	E	
15	E	35	B			15	C	35	D	
16	D	36	D			16	D	36	B	
17	B	37	A			17	C	37	C	
18	B	38	E			18	E	38	D	
19	B	39	E			19	B	39	A	
20	E	40	B			20	D	40	E	

	CBEST Practice Test 3						CBEST Practice Test 4				
1	C	21	C	41	D	1	D	21	E	41	B
2	E	22	B	42	A	2	C	22	D	42	B
3	D	23	C	43	D	3	E	23	B	43	C
4	E	24	D	44	B	4	D	24	D	44	B
5	E	25	E	45	D	5	E	25	A	45	D
6	D	26	B	46	D	6	C	26	B	46	B
7	D	27	D	47	A	7	C	27	C	47	D
8	E	28	E	48	A	8	A	28	E	48	D
9	A	29	D	49	C	9	B	29	D	49	A
10	C	30	B	50	B	10	D	30	B	50	E
11	E	31	D			11	D	31	A		
12	E	32	E			12	E	32	D		
13	C	33	C			13	A	33	C		
14	A	34	D			14	D	34	C		
15	B	35	B			15	B	35	C		
16	A	36	C			16	D	36	D		
17	D	37	E			17	A	37	D		
18	E	38	E			18	B	38	A		
19	D	39	D			19	C	39	E		
20	E	40	E			20	A	40	E		

CBEST Practice Test 5

1	A	21	A	41	E
2	B	22	D	42	C
3	A	23	E	43	D
4	B	24	A	44	D
5	D	25	B	45	D
6	B	26	D	46	E
7	C	27	D	47	A
8	B	28	E	48	C
9	C	29	B	49	D
10	C	30	E	50	E
11	B	31	E		
12	C	32	B		
13	B	33	B		
14	C	34	E		
15	A	35	C		
16	C	36	C		
17	C	37	D		
18	B	38	C		
19	C	39	A		
20	D	40	B		

CBEST Mathematics Practice Tests Answers and Explanations

CBEST Mathematics Practice Test 1 Explanations

1) Choice C is correct

Add the first 5 numbers. $40 + 45 + 50 + 35 + 55 = 225$, To find the distance traveled in the next 5 hours, multiply the average by number of hours.

$Distance = Average \times Rate = 65 \times 5 = 325$. Add both numbers. $325 + 225 = 550$

2) Choice C is correct

Use distance formula: $Distance = Rate \times time \Rightarrow 420 = 50 \times T$, divide both sides by $50. 420 \div 50 = T \Rightarrow T = 8.4\ hours$. Change hours to minutes for the decimal part. $0.4\ hours = 0.4 \times 60 = 24\ minutes$.

3) Choice D is correct

Smallest 5–digit number is $10,000$, and biggest 5–digit number is $99,999$. The difference is: $89,999$.

4) Choice C is correct

There are 6 spaces, so first divide 140 by 6: $140 \div 6 = 23$ remainder 2. So, the arrow goes around 23 full circle and then 2 more spaces.

Two spaces from Space O is Space Q.

5) Choice D is correct

Use Pythagorean Theorem: $a^2 + b^2 = c^2 \Rightarrow 5^2 + 12^2 = c^2 \Rightarrow 169 = c^2 \Rightarrow c = 13$

6) Choice E is correct

3.5% of $1,200$ is: $0.035 \times 1,200 = 42$

7) Choice E is correct

Use distributive property: $5x(4 + 2y) = 20x + 10xy$

8) Choice D is correct

$y = 5ab + 3b^3$. Plug in the values of a and b in the equation: $a = 2$ and $b = 3$.

$y = 5(2)(3) + 3(3)^3 = 30 + 3(27) = 30 + 81 = 111$

9) Choice C is correct

$x = \frac{15}{20} = 0.75$ converting 0.75 to percent we have: $0.75 = 75\%$. Then 15 is 75% of 20.

10) Choice E is correct

The perimeter of the trapezoid is 64. Therefore, the missing side (height) is:

$64 - 18 - 12 - 14 = 20$. Area of the trapezoid:

$$A = \frac{1}{2}h(b_1 + b_2) = \frac{1}{2}(20\ cm)(12\ cm + 14\ cm) = 260\ cm^2$$

11) Choice C is correct

Let x be the number. Write the equation and solve for x. $\frac{2}{3} \times 15 = \frac{2}{5}x \Rightarrow \frac{2 \times 15}{3} = \frac{2x}{5}$, use cross multiplication to solve for x. $5 \times 30 = 2x \times 3 \Rightarrow 150 = 6x \Rightarrow x = 25$

12) Choice C is correct

To find the discount, multiply the number by $(100\% - rate\ of\ discount)$.

Therefore, for the first discount we get: $(D)(100\% - 25\%) = (D)(0.75) = 0.75\ D$

For increase of 20%: $(0.75\ D)(100\% + 20\%) = (0.75\ D)(1.20) = 0.90\ D = 90\%\ of\ D$

13) Choice B is correct

Write the numbers in order: $1, 5, 8, 10, 13, 15, 18$. Since we have 7 numbers (7 is odd), then the median is the number in the middle, which is 10.

14) Choice E is correct

Surface Area of a cylinder $= 2\pi r(r + h)$, The radius of the cylinder is 8 inches and its height is 14 inches. Surface Area of a cylinder $= 2(\pi)(8)(8 + 14) = 352\pi$

15) Choice E is correct

$$average = \frac{sum\ of\ terms}{number\ of\ terms} \Rightarrow 20 = \frac{13 + 15 + 20 + x}{4} \Rightarrow 80 = 48 + x \Rightarrow x = 32$$

16) Choice D is correct

Let x be the original price. If the price of the sofa is decreased by 25% to $450, then: 75% of $x = 450 \Rightarrow 0.75x = 450 \Rightarrow x = 450 \div 0.75 = 600$

17) Choice B is correct

Use the formula of areas of circles. $Area = \pi r^2 \Rightarrow 49\pi = \pi r^2 \Rightarrow 49 = r^2 \Rightarrow r = 7$

Radius of the circle is 7. Now, use the circumference formula:

Circumference $= 2\pi r = 2\pi(7) = 14\pi$.

18) Choice B is correct

Use the formula for Percent of Change. $\frac{New\ Value - Old\ Value}{Old\ Value} \times 100\% \Rightarrow$

$$\frac{28 - 50}{50} \times 100\ \% = -44\%$$

(negative sign here means that the new price is less than old price).

19) Choice B is correct

The question is this: 1.75 is what percent of 1.40? Use percent formula:

$$part = \frac{percent}{100} \times whole \Rightarrow 1.75 = \frac{percent}{100} \times 1.40 \Rightarrow 1.75 = \frac{percent \times 1.40}{100} \Rightarrow$$

$$175 = percent \times 1.40 \Rightarrow percent = \frac{175}{1.40} = 125$$

20) Choice E is correct

Use the information provided in the question to draw the shape.

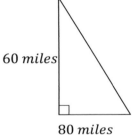

60 *miles*

80 *miles*

Use Pythagorean Theorem: $a^2 + b^2 = c^2$

$60^2 + 80^2 = c^2 \Rightarrow 3,600 + 6,400 = c^2 \Rightarrow 10,000 = c^2 \Rightarrow c = 100$

21) Choice E is correct

Some of prime numbers are: 2, 3, 5, 7, 11, 13. Find the product of two consecutive prime numbers: $2 \times 3 = 6$ (not in the options), $3 \times 5 = 15$ (not in the options!), $5 \times 7 = 35$ (bingo!).

22) Choice B is correct

The question is this: 530.40 is what percent of 624?

$$percent = \frac{530.40}{624} \times 100 = 85.$$

530.40 is 85% of 624. Therefore, the discount is: $100\% - 85\% = 15\%$

23) Choice A is correct

If the score of Mia was 40, therefore the score of Ava is 20. Since, the score of Emma was half as that of Ava, therefore, the score of Emma is 10.

24) Choice E is correct

If 17 balls are removed from the bag at random, there will be one ball in the bag. The probability of choosing a brown ball is 1 out of 18. Therefore, the probability of not choosing a brown ball is 17 out of 18 and the probability of having not a brown ball after removing 17 balls is the same.

25) Choice C is correct

Let x be the smallest number. Then, these are the numbers:

$x, x + 1, x + 2, x + 3, x + 4$

$average = \frac{sum\ of\ terms}{number\ of\ terms} \Rightarrow 36 = \frac{x+(x+1)+(x+2)+(x+3)+(x+4)}{5} \Rightarrow 36 = \frac{5x+10}{5} \Rightarrow$

$180 = 5x + 10 \Rightarrow 170 = 5x \Rightarrow x = 34$

26) Choice C is correct

Use this formula: $Percent\ of\ Change = \frac{New\ Value - Old\ Value}{Old\ Value} \times 100\%$

$\frac{18,200-28,000}{28,000} \times 100\% = -35\%$. The negative sign means that the price decreased.

27) Choice D is correct

If the length of the box is 36, then the width of the box is one third of it, 12, and the height of the box is 4 (one third of the width). The volume of the box is:

$V = lwh = (36)(12)(4) = 1,728$

28) Choice C is correct

Write the equation and solve for B: $0.60A = 0.30B$, divide both sides by 0.30, then you will have $\frac{0.60}{0.30}A = B$, therefore: $B = 2A$, and B is 2 times of A or it's 200% of A.

29) Choice E is correct

To find the number of possible outfit combinations, multiply number of options for each factor: $4 \times 3 \times 5 = 60$

30) Choice D is correct

The sum of supplement angles is 180. Let x be that angle. Therefore, $x + 9x = 180$

$10x = 180$, divide both sides by 10: $x = 18$

31) Choice A is correct

The percent of girls playing tennis is: $40\% \times 25\% = 0.40 \times 0.25 = 0.1 \rightarrow 10\%$

32) Choice D is correct

The area of the floor is: $7 cm \times 24\ cm = 168\ cm^2$.

The number is tiles needed $= 168 \div 8 = 21$.

33) Choice C is correct

The weight of 14.2 meters of this rope is: $14.2 \times 600\ g = 8,520\ g$

$1\ kg = 1,000\ g$, therefore, $8,520\ g \div 1,000 = 8.52\ kg$

34) Choice B is correct

6% of the volume of the solution is alcohol. Let x be the volume of the solution.

Then: 6% of $x = 24\ ml \Rightarrow 0.06x = 24 \Rightarrow x = 24 \div 0.06 = 400$

35) Choice B is correct

$average = \frac{sum\ of\ terms}{number\ of\ terms}$. The sum of the weight of all girls is: $18 \times 56 = 1,008\ kg$

The sum of the weight of all boys is: $32 \times 62 = 1,984\ kg$. The sum of the weight of all students is: $1,008 + 1,984 = 2,992\ kg$ $average = \frac{2,992}{50} = 59.84$

36) Choice D is correct

Let x be the original price. If the price of a laptop is decreased by 20% to \$360, then: 80% of $x = 360 \Rightarrow 0.80x = 360 \Rightarrow x = 360 \div 0.80 = 450$

37) Choice A is correct

$(2.9 \times 10^6) \times (2.6 \times 10^{-5}) = (2.9 \times 2.6) \times (10^6 \times 10^{-5}) = 7.54 \times (10^{6+(-5)}) \Rightarrow$

7.54×10^1

38) Choice E is correct

The formula of the volume of pyramid is: $V = \frac{l \times w \times h}{3}$

The length and width of the pyramid is $6\ cm$ and its height is $12\ cm$. Therefore:

$V = \frac{6 \times 6 \times 14}{3} = 168\ cm^3$

39) Choice E is correct

Since the triangle ABC is reflected over the y-axis, then all values of y's of the points don't change and the sign of all x's change. (remember that when a point is reflected over the y-axis, the value of y does not change and when a point is reflected over the

x-axis, the value of x does not change). Therefore:$(-1, 4)$ changes to $(1, 4)$,$(-2, 5)$ changes to $(2, 5)$,$(5, 9)$ changes to $(-5, 9)$.

40) Choice B is correct

Use Pythagorean theorem: $a^2 + b^2 = c^2 \rightarrow 8^2 + 6^2 = x^2 \rightarrow 64 + 36 = x^2 \rightarrow 100 = x^2 \rightarrow$

$x = 10\,ft$

41) Choice D is correct

$(11 \times 36) + (6 \times 12) + 6 = 474$

42) Choice A is correct

Let x be the integer. Then: $2x - 5 = 73$, Add 5 both sides: $2x = 78$, Divide both sides by 2: $x = 39$

43) Choice C is correct

To find the discount, multiply the number by $(100\% - rate\ of\ discount)$. Therefore, for the first discount we get: $(300)(100\% - 15\%) = (300)(0.85)$. For the next 15% discount: $(300)(0.85)(0.85)$.

44) Choice E is correct

Use PEMDAS (order of operation):

$6 + 8 \times (-2) - [4 + 22 \times 5] \div 6 = 6 + 8 \times (-2) - [4 + 110] \div 6 =$

$6 + 8 \times (-2) - [114] \div 6 = 6 + (-16) - 19 = 6 + (-16) - 19 = -10 - 19 = -29$

45) Choice B is correct

Call the missing angle in the top half of the figure y. The sum of the four angles on the top of the figure is equal to 180°: $x + y + 50 + 60 = 180$

Since y is a vertical angle with the $45°$ angle, then y is also 45°. Use that to solve for x: $45 + x + 50 + 60 = 180 \rightarrow 155 + x = 180 \rightarrow x = 25°$

46) Choice D is correct

$Average = \frac{Sum\ of\ Terms}{Number\ of\ Terms} \rightarrow Average = \frac{157 + 164 + 148 + 167 + 171 + 159}{6} = \frac{966}{6} = 161$

47) Choice B is correct

Ratio of women to men in city A: $\frac{570}{600} = 0.95$

Ratio of women to men in city B: $\frac{291}{300} = 0.97$

Ratio of women to men in city C: $\frac{665}{700} = 0.95$

Ratio of women to men in city D: $\frac{528}{550} = 0.96$

Choice B is the maximum number.

48) Choice E is correct

Percentage of men in city $A = \frac{600}{1,170} \times 100 \approx 51.28\%$

Percentage of women in city $C = \frac{665}{1,365} \times 100 \approx 48.72\%$

Percentage of men in city A to percentage of women in city $C = \frac{51.28}{48.72} = 1.05$

(Notice that $\frac{51.28}{48.72}$ is bigger than 1 and only choice E is bigger than 1)

49) Choice D is correct

Let the number of women should be added to city D be x, then:

$\frac{528+x}{550} = 1.2 \rightarrow 528 + x = 550 \times 1.2 \rightarrow 528 + x = 660 \rightarrow x = 132$

50) Choice D is correct

Let x be all expenses, then $\frac{22}{100}x = \$660 \rightarrow x = \frac{100 \times \$660}{22} = \$3,000$

He spent for his rent: $\frac{27}{100} \times \$3,000 = \$810$

CBEST Mathematics Practice Test 2 Explanations

1) Choice D is correct

$average\ (mean) = \frac{sum\ of\ terms}{number\ of\ terms} \Rightarrow 90 = \frac{sum\ of\ terms}{50} \Rightarrow sum = 90 \times 50 = 4,500$

The difference of 94 and 69 is 25. Therefore, 25 should be subtracted from the sum.

$4,500 - 25 = 4,475, mean = \frac{sum\ of\ terms}{number\ of\ terms} \Rightarrow mean = \frac{4,475}{50} = 89.5$

2) Choice B is correct

For sum of 5: (1 & 4) and (4 & 1), (2 & 3) and (3 & 2), therefore we have 4 options.

For sum of 8: (5 & 3) and (3 & 5), (4 & 4) and (2 & 6), and (6 & 2), we have 5 options. To get a sum of 5 or 8 for two dice: $4 + 5 = 9$. Since, we have $6 \times 6 = 36$ total number of options, the probability of getting a sum of 5 and 8 is 9 out of 36 or $\frac{9}{36} = \frac{1}{4}$

3) Choice B is correct

First, find the angles α and β. Angles 112 and α are supplementary. Then:

$a + 112 = 180 \rightarrow \alpha = 180° - 112° = 68°$

Angles 135 and β are also supplementary. $\beta = 180° - 135° = 45°$

The sum of all angles in a triangle is 180 degrees. Then:

$x + \alpha + \beta = 180° \rightarrow x = 180° - 68° - 45° = 67°$

4) Choice D is correct

Plug in the value of x and y. $x = 3$ and $y = -2$.

$6(x - 2y) + (2 - x)^2 = 6(3 - 2(-2)) + (2 - 3)^2 = 6(3 + 4) + (-1)^2 = 42 + 1 = 43$

5) Choice D is correct

Use formula of rectangle prism volume. $V = (length)(width)(height) \Rightarrow$

$2,500 = (25)(10)(height) \Rightarrow height = 2,500 \div 250 = 10\ feet$

6) Choice D is correct

To find the number of possible outfit combinations, multiply number of options for each factor: $2 \times 5 \times 4 = 40$

7) Choice C is correct

$$4 \div \frac{1}{3} = 12$$

8) Choice B is correct

The diagonal of the square is 4. Let x be the side. Use Pythagorean Theorem: $a^2 + b^2 = c^2$

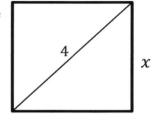

$$x^2 + x^2 = 4^2 \Rightarrow 2x^2 = 4^2 \Rightarrow 2x^2 = 16 \Rightarrow x^2 = 8 \Rightarrow x = \sqrt{8}$$

The area of the square is: $\sqrt{8} \times \sqrt{8} = 8$

9) Choice A is correct

$AB = 5$ and $BC = 12$, $AC = \sqrt{12^2 + 5^2} = \sqrt{144 + 25} = \sqrt{169} = 13$

Perimeter $= 5 + 12 + 13 = 30$, Area $= \frac{5 \times 12}{2} = 5 \times 6 = 30$

In this case, the ratio of the perimeter of the triangle to its area is: $\frac{30}{30} = 1$

If the sides AB and BC become twice longer, then: $AB = 10$ And $BC = 24$

$$AC = \sqrt{24^2 + 10^2} = \sqrt{576 + 100} = \sqrt{676} = 26$$

Perimeter $= 26 + 24 + 10 = 60$, Area $= \frac{10 \times 24}{2} = 10 \times 12 = 120$

In this case the ratio of the perimeter of the triangle to its area is: $\frac{60}{120} = \frac{1}{2}$

10) Choice D is correct

Solve for the sum of five numbers.

$$average = \frac{sum\ of\ terms}{number\ of\ terms} \Rightarrow 26 = \frac{sum\ of\ 5\ numbers}{5} \Rightarrow sum\ of\ 5\ numbers = 26 \times 5 = 130$$

The sum of 5 numbers is 130. If a sixth number 42 is added, then the sum of 6 numbers is $130 + 42 = 172 \Rightarrow average = \frac{sum\ of\ terms}{number\ of\ terms} = \frac{172}{6} = 28.67$

11) Choice C is correct

2,500 out of 65,000 equals to $\frac{2,500}{65,000} = \frac{25}{650} = \frac{1}{26}$

12) Choice A is correct

Let x be the number of shoes the team can purchase. Therefore, the team can purchase $110x$. The team had $20,000 and spent $14,000. Now the team can spend on new shoes $6,000 at most. Now, write the inequality: $110x + 14,000 \leq 20,000$

13) Choice E is correct

Jason needs an 70% average to pass for five exams. Therefore, the sum of 5 exams must be at least $5 \times 70 = 350$. The sum of 4 exams is: $68 + 72 + 85 + 90 = 315$

The minimum score Jason can earn on his fifth and final test to pass is:

$350 - 315 = 35$

14) Choice B is correct

Set up a proportion to solve.

$$\frac{1\frac{1}{7} \, in}{\frac{1}{5} \, yr} = \frac{x \, in}{1 \, yr} \rightarrow 1\frac{1}{7} = \frac{1}{5}x \rightarrow \frac{8}{7} = \frac{1}{5}x \rightarrow \left(\frac{5}{1}\right)\left(\frac{8}{7}\right) = x \rightarrow x = \frac{40}{7} \rightarrow x = 5\frac{5}{7}$$

15) Choice C is correct

The rate of construction company $= \frac{30 \, cm}{1 \, min} = 30 \frac{cm}{min}$

The height of the wall after 40 minutes $= \frac{30 \, cm}{1 \, min} \times 40 \, min = 1,200 \, cm$

Let x be the height of wall, then $\frac{3}{4}x = 1,200 \, cm \rightarrow x = \frac{4 \times 1,200}{3} \rightarrow x = 1,600 \, cm = 16 \, m$

16) Choice D is correct

If Kim's earning $= 100\%$, then, John's earning is 90% of Kim's earning. Then:

$0.90 \times 55 = 49.50$

17) Choice C is correct

Three times of 25,000 is 75,000. One sixth of them cancelled their tickets. One sixth of 75,000 equals 12,500 $\left(\frac{1}{6} \times 75,000 = 12,500\right)$. 62,500 $(75,000 - 12,500 = 62,500)$ fans are attending this week.

18) Choice E is correct

The area of the square is 49 inches. Therefore, the side of the square is square root of the area: $\sqrt{49} = 7$ inches.

Four times the side of the square is the perimeter: $4 \times 7 = 28 \, inches$

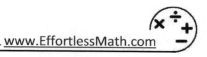

19) Choice B is correct

Since, E is the midpoint of AB, then the area of all triangles DAE, DEF, CFE and CBE are equal. Let x be the area of one of the triangles, Then: $4x = 100 \rightarrow x = 25$

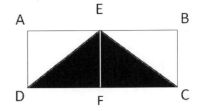

The area of $DEC = 2x = 2(25) = 50$

20) Choice D is correct

The integers that are included in Set A but not in Set B are 15 through 73. (Note that 74 is included in Set B). To calculate the number of integers between 15 and 73, inclusive, subtract the two endpoints and add 1. (One must be added because the endpoints are both counted in the total) $73 - 15 + 1 = 59$

21) Choice E is correct

Since the ordered pair is reflected over the x-axis, then, the value of x of the point doesn't change and the sign of y changes. $(-4, 5) \Rightarrow (-4, -5)$

22) Choice E is correct

To find the answer, multiply 12 by 23 and add the result to 19:

$(12 \times 23) + 19 = 295$

23) Choice C is correct

$\$9 \times 10 = \$90$, Petrol use: $10 \times 2 = 20$ liters

Petrol cost: $20 \times \$1 = \$20$, Money earned: $\$90 - \$20 = \$70$

24) Choice C is correct

Use the information provided in the question to draw the shape.

Use Pythagorean Theorem: $a^2 + b^2 = c^2$

$50^2 + 120^2 = c^2 \Rightarrow 2,500 + 14,400 = c^2 \Rightarrow c^2 = 16,900 \Rightarrow$

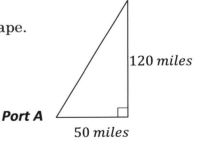

$c = 130\ miles$

25) Choice B is correct

Plug in 104 for F and then solve for C.

$C = \dfrac{5}{9}(F - 32) \Rightarrow C = \dfrac{5}{9}(104 - 32) \Rightarrow C = \dfrac{5}{9}(72) = 40$

26) Choice C is correct

$$Probability = \frac{number\ of\ desired\ outcomes}{number\ of\ total\ outcomes} = \frac{10}{15+10+10+25} = \frac{10}{60} = \frac{1}{6}$$

27) Choice E is correct

Find the difference of each pairs of numbers: $3, 4, 6, 9, 13, 18, 24, \_\_, 39$

The difference of 3 and 4 is 1, 4 and 6 is 2, 6 and 9 is 3, 9 and 13 is 4, 13 and 18 is 5, 18 and 24 is 6, 24 and next number should be 7. The number is $24 + 7 = 31$

28) Choice A is correct

The width of the rectangle is twice its length. Let x be the length. Then, $width = 2x$

Perimeter of the rectangle is $2(width + length) = 2(2x + x) = 72 \Rightarrow 6x = 72 \Rightarrow$

$x = 12$. Length of the rectangle is 12 meters.

29) Choice D is correct

First, simplify the inequality: $x + 5 < 21 \to x < 16$

The positive integers that satisfy the inequality are $1, 2, 3, ..., 14, 15$. (We cannot include 16 because x must be less than 16) 15 positive integers satisfy this inequality.

30) Choice C is correct

Volume of a box $= length \times width \times height = 3 \times 5 \times 6 = 90$

31) Choice B is correct

The population is increased by 10% and 20%. 10% increase changes the population to 110% of original population. For the second increase, multiply the result by 120%.

$(1.10) \times (1.20) = 1.32 = 132\%$.

32 percent of the population is increased after two years.

32) Choice D is correct

The smallest number is -15. To find the largest possible value of one of the other five integers, we need to choose the smallest possible integers for four of them. Let x be the largest number. Then: $-70 = (-15) + (-14) + (-13) + (-12) + (-11) + x \to$ $-70 = -65 + x \to x = -70 + 65 = -5$

33) Choice D is correct

If 20% of a number is 4, what is the number: 20% of $x = 4 \Rightarrow 0.20x = 4 \Rightarrow$

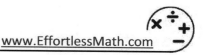

$x = 4 \div 0.20 = 20$

34) Choice E is correct

$12 is what percent of $40? → $12 \div 40 = 0.30 = 30\%$

35) Choice D is correct

15% of $160 is $0.15 \times 160 = 24$

36) Choice B is correct

A is 4 times of B, then: $A = 4B \Rightarrow (A = 12) 12 = 4 \times B \Rightarrow B = 12 \div 4 = 3$

37) Choice C is correct

The distance between Jason and Joe is 9 *miles*. Jason running at 6.5 *miles per hour* and Joe is running at the speed of 8 *miles per hour*. Therefore, every hour the distance is 1.5 *miles* less. $9 \div 1.5 = 6$ *hours*

38) Choice D is correct

The failing rate is 11 out of $44 = \frac{11}{44}$, Change the fraction to percent: $\frac{11}{44} \times 100\% = 25\%$. 25 percent of students failed. Therefore, 75 percent of students passed the exam.

39) Choice A is correct

The length of MN is equal to: $3x + 5x = 8x$. Then: $8x = 40 \rightarrow x = \frac{40}{8} = 5$

The length of ON is equal to: $5x = 5 \times 5 = 25$ *cm*

40) Choice E is correct

Let x be the width of the rectangle. Use Pythagorean Theorem:

$a^2 + b^2 = c^2$

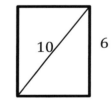

$x^2 + 6^2 = 10^2 \Rightarrow x^2 + 36 = 100 \Rightarrow x^2 = 100 - 36 \Rightarrow x^2 = 64 \Rightarrow x = 8$

Perimeter of the rectangle $= 2(length + width) = 2(8 + 6) = 2(14) = 28$

41) Choice D is correct

Plug in the value of $x = 30$ into both equations. Then:

$C(x) = x^2 + 2x = (30)^2 + 2(30) = 900 + 60 = 960.$

$R(x) = 40x = 40 \times 30 = 1{,}200 \rightarrow 1{,}200 - 960 = 240$

The profit of producing 30 textbooks is $240.

42) Choice C is correct

Angles AOD and DOC are complementary angles. Therefore, their sum is 90 degrees. Then:

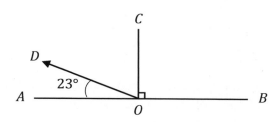

$$DOC + AOD = 90° \rightarrow DOC = 90 - AOD \rightarrow$$

$$DOC = 90 - 23 = 67$$

43) Choice B is correct

The probability of choosing a Hearts is: $\frac{13}{52} = \frac{1}{4}$

44) Choice D is correct

Change the numbers to decimal and then compare.

$\frac{1}{3} = 0.\bar{3}$, 0.68, $67\% = 0.67$, $\frac{4}{5} = 0.80$

Therefore $\frac{1}{3} < 67\% < 0.68 < \frac{4}{5}$

45) Choice B is correct

Round both numbers, then multiply: $3,689 \times 340 \rightarrow 4,000 \times 300 = 1,200,000$

46) Choice D is correct

First, find the relationship between y and x. Based on the values provided in the table, the relationship between y and x is: $y = 1.5x$. Now, find the missing y by substituting the value of x in the equation. Then: $y = 1.5x \rightarrow y = 1.5 \times 3.5 = 5.25$

47) Choice B is correct

$Percent = \frac{part}{whole} \times 100 = \frac{18}{18+33+26+13} \times 100 = \frac{18}{90} \times 100 = 20\%$

48) Choice D is correct

Number of sixth grade of students $= 18 + 27 = 45$

Number of sixth grade girls students $= 27$

$Percent = \frac{part}{whole} \times 100 \rightarrow Percent = \frac{27}{45} \times 100 = 60\%$

49) Choice D is correct

Let x be the number of purple marbles. Let's review the choices provided:

A. $\frac{1}{10}$, if the probability of choosing a purple marble is one out of ten, then:

$$Probability = \frac{number\ of\ desired\ outcomes}{number\ of\ total\ outcomes} = \frac{x}{20+30+40+x} = \frac{1}{10}$$

Use cross multiplication and solve for x. $10x = 90 + x \rightarrow 9x = 90 \rightarrow x = 10$

Since the number of purple marbles can be 10, then, choice A can be the probability of randomly selecting a purple marble from the bag. Use the same method for other choices.

B. $\frac{1}{4} \rightarrow \frac{x}{20+30+40+x} = \frac{1}{4} \rightarrow 4x = 90 + x \rightarrow 3x = 90 \rightarrow x = 30$

C. $\frac{2}{5} \rightarrow \frac{x}{20+30+40+x} = \frac{2}{5} \rightarrow 5x = 180 + 2x \rightarrow 3x = 180 \rightarrow x = 60$

D. $\frac{7}{15} \rightarrow \frac{x}{20+30+40+x} = \frac{7}{15} \rightarrow 15x = 630 + 7x \rightarrow 8x = 630 \rightarrow x = 78.75$

E. $\frac{9}{15} \rightarrow \frac{x}{20+30+40+x} = \frac{9}{15} \rightarrow 15x = 810 + 9x \rightarrow 6x = 810 \rightarrow x = 135$

Number of purple marbles cannot be a decimal. Therefore, Choice D can NOT be the probability of randomly selecting a purple marble from the bag.

50) Choice D is correct

Of the 30 employees, there are 5 females under age 45 and 6 males age 45 or older. Therefore, the probability that the person selected will be either a female under age 45 or a male age 45 or older is: $\frac{5}{30} + \frac{6}{30} = \frac{11}{30}$

CBEST Mathematics Practice Test 3 Explanations

1) Choice C is correct

The area of the trapezoid is:

$$Area = \frac{1}{2}h(b_1 + b_2) \rightarrow 126 = \frac{1}{2}(x)(13 + 8) \rightarrow 126 = 10.5x \rightarrow x = 12$$

$$y = \sqrt{5^2 + 12^2} = \sqrt{25 + 144} = \sqrt{169} = 13$$

The perimeter of the trapezoid is: $12 + 13 + 8 + 13 = 46$

2) Choice E is correct

First calculate the number of feet that 1 inch represents: $100\ ft \div 5\ in = 20\ ft/in$

Then multiply this by the total number of inches: $18\ in \times 20\ ft/in = 360\ ft$

3) Choice D is correct

Let's compare each fraction: $\frac{2}{7} < \frac{3}{8} < \frac{5}{11} < \frac{3}{4}$

Only choice D provides the right order.

4) Choice E is correct

$6^4 = 6 \times 6 \times 6 \times 6 = 1,296$

5) Choice E is correct

If each book weighs $\frac{1}{5}$ pound, then 1 pound = 5 books. To find the number of books in 50 pounds, simply multiply this 5 by 50: $50 \times 5 = 250$

6) Choice D is correct

Use the volume of square pyramid formula.

$$V = \frac{1}{3}a^2h \Rightarrow V = \frac{1}{3}(12\ m)^2 \times 10\ m \Rightarrow V = 480\ m^3$$

7) Choice D is correct

Isolate and solve for x: $\frac{2}{3}x + \frac{1}{6} = \frac{1}{3} \Rightarrow \frac{2}{3}x = \frac{1}{3} - \frac{1}{6} \Rightarrow \frac{2}{3}x = \frac{1}{6}$

Multiply both sides by the reciprocal of the coefficient of x.

$$\left(\frac{3}{2}\right)\frac{2}{3}x = \frac{1}{6}\left(\frac{3}{2}\right) \Rightarrow x = \frac{3}{12} = \frac{1}{4}$$

8) Choice E is correct

The area of the circle is 16π, then, its diameter is 8.

Area of a circle $= \pi r^2 = 16\pi \to r^2 = 16 \to r = 4$

Radius of the circle is 4 and diameter is twice of it, 8.

One side of the square equals to the diameter of the circle. Then:

$Area\ of\ square = side \times side = 8 \times 8 = 64$

9) Choice A is correct

The median of a set of data is the value located in the middle of the data set. Combine the two sets provided, and organize them in increasing order:

$\{1, 3, 4, 6, 8, 10, 12, 14, 15, 17\}$

Since there are 10 numbers (an even number of items) in the resulting list, the median is the average of the two middle numbers. Median $= \frac{(8+10)}{2} = 9$

10) Choice C is correct

The area of the non-shaded region is equal to the area of the bigger rectangle subtracted by the area of smaller rectangle.

Area of the bigger rectangle $= 12 \times 16 = 192$

Area of the smaller rectangle $= 10 \times 4 = 40$

Area of the non-shaded region $= 192 - 40 = 152$

11) Choice E is correct

In the figure angle A is labeled $(3x - 2)$ and it measures 37. Thus, $3x - 2 = 37$ and $3x = 39$ or $x = 13$. That means that angle B, which is labeled $(5x)$, must measure $5 \times 13 = 65$.

Since the three angles of a triangle must add up to 180,

$37 + 65 + y - 8 = 180$, then: $y + 94 = 180 \to y = 180 - 94 = 86$

12) Choice E is correct

Let x be total number of cards in the box, then number of red cards is: $x - 246$

The probability of choosing a red card is one third. Then: $probability = \frac{1}{3} = \frac{x-246}{x}$

Use cross multiplication to solve for x.

$$x \times 1 = 3(x - 246) \rightarrow x = 3x - 738 \rightarrow 2x = 738 \rightarrow x = 369$$

13) Choice C is correct

y is the intersection of the three circles. Therefore, it must be odd (from circle A), negative (from circle B), and multiple of 5 (from circle C).

From the choices provided, only -5 is odd, negative and multiple of 5.

14) Choice A is correct

An obtuse angle is an angle of greater than 90 degrees and less than 180 degrees. Only choice A is an obtuse angle.

15) Choice B is correct

Recall that the formula for the average is: $Average = \dfrac{sum\ of\ data}{number\ of\ data}$

First, compute the total weight of all balls in the basket: $25\ g = \dfrac{total\ weight}{20\ balls}$

$total\ weight = 25\ g \times 20 \rightarrow total\ weight = 500\ g$.

Next, find the total weight of the 5 largest marbles:

$$40\ g = \dfrac{total\ weight}{5\ balls} \rightarrow total\ weight = 40\ g \times 5 \rightarrow total\ weight = 200\ g$$

The total weight of the heaviest balls is $200\ g$. Then, the total weight of the remaining 15 balls is $300\ g$: $500\ g - 200\ g = 300\ g$.

The average weight of the remaining balls: $Average = \dfrac{300\ g}{15\ balls} = 20\ g$ per ball

16) Choice A is correct

In the stadium the ratio of home fans to visiting fans in a crowd is $5 : 7$. Therefore, total number of fans must be divisible by 12: $5 + 7 = 12$.

Let's review the choices:

A. $12,324 \rightarrow 12,324 \div 12 = 1,027$

B. $42,326 \rightarrow 42,326 \div 12 = 3,527.1\overline{6}$

C. $44,566 \rightarrow 44,566 \div 12 = 3,713.8\overline{3}$

D. $66,812 \rightarrow 66,812 \div 12 = 5,567.\overline{6}$

E. $69,752 \rightarrow 69,752 \div 12 = 5,812.\overline{6}$

Only choice A when divided by 12 results a whole number.

17) Choice D is correct

Fist convert mixed numbers to fractions: $2\frac{2}{3} - 1\frac{5}{6} = 2\frac{4}{6} - 1\frac{5}{6} = \frac{16}{6} - \frac{11}{6} = \frac{5}{6}$

18) Choice E is correct

$x = \frac{1}{3}$ and $y = \frac{9}{21}$, substitute the values of x and y in the expression and simplify:

$\frac{1}{x} \div \frac{y}{3} \rightarrow \frac{1}{\frac{1}{3}} \div \frac{\frac{9}{21}}{3} \rightarrow \frac{1}{\frac{1}{3}} = 3$ and $\frac{\frac{9}{21}}{3} = \frac{9}{63} = \frac{1}{7}$. Then: $\frac{1}{\frac{1}{3}} \div \frac{\frac{9}{21}}{3} = 3 \div \frac{1}{7} = 3 \times 7 = 21$

19) Choice D is correct

Let E age of Ella, we know Ella is 4 years older than Ava: $E = 4 + A \rightarrow A = S - 3$

20) Choice E is correct

Let x be the number of current stamps in the collection. Then:

$$\frac{6}{5}x - x = 100 \rightarrow \frac{1}{5}x = 100 \rightarrow x = 500$$

50% more of 500 is: $500 + 0.50 \times 500 = 500 + 250 = 750$.

21) Choice C is correct

The sum of 8 numbers is greater than 240 and less than 320. Then, the average of the 8 numbers must be greater than 30 and less than 40.

$\frac{240}{8} < x < \frac{320}{8} \rightarrow 30 < x < 40$

The only choice that is between 30 and 40 is 35.

22) Choice B is correct

The angles on a straight line add up to 180 degrees. Then: $x + 25 + y + 2x + y = 180$

Then, $3x + 2y = 180 - 25 \rightarrow 3(35) + 2y = 155 \rightarrow 2y = 155 - 105 \rightarrow 2y = 50 \rightarrow y = 25$

23) Choice C is correct

Let L be the length of the rectangular and W be the width of the rectangular. Then,

$L = 4W + 3$

The perimeter of the rectangle is 36 meters. Therefore: $2L + 2W = 36, L + W = 18$

Replace the value of L from the first equation into the second equation and solve for W: $(4W + 3) + W = 18 \rightarrow 5W + 3 = 18 \rightarrow 5W = 15 \rightarrow W = 3$

The width of the rectangle is 3 meters and its length is: $L = 4W + 3 = 4(3) + 3 = 15$

The area of the rectangle is: $Length \times Width = 3 \times 15 = 45$

24) Choice D is correct

First, find the measure of angle RQS. Angles RQS and PQR are supplementary and therefore their sum is 180 degrees. Then:

$PQR + RQS = 180 \rightarrow 135 + RQS = 180 \rightarrow RQS = 45$

The sum of all angles in a triangle is 180 degrees. Then:

$45 + 52 + x = 180 \rightarrow 97 + x = 180 \rightarrow x = 83$

25) Choice E is correct

The sum of two supplementary angles is 180 degrees. Then:

$(3x - 10) + (x + 2) = 180$. Simplify and solve for x: $(3x - 10) + (x + 2) = 180 \rightarrow$

$4x - 8 = 180 \rightarrow 4x = 180 + 8 \rightarrow 4x = 188 \rightarrow x = 47$

26) Choice B is correct

To find the area of the shaded region subtract the area of the smaller circle from bigger circle.

$$S_{bigger} - S_{smaller} = \pi \left(r_{bigger}\right)^2 - \pi (r_{smaller})^2 \Rightarrow$$

$$S_{bigger} - S_{smaller} = \pi(6)^2 - \pi(4)^2 \Rightarrow 36\pi - 16\pi = 20\pi \ in^2$$

27) Choice D is correct

$$\frac{a + b}{2} = \frac{a}{2} + \frac{b}{2}$$

28) Choice E is correct

$2.5\% \ of \ 1,200 = \frac{2.5}{100} \times 1,200 = 30$

29) Choice D is correct

Solve for x: $x^3 + 18 = 130 \rightarrow x^3 = 112$

Let's review the choices.

A. 1 and 2 $\quad$ $1^3 = 1$ and $2^3 = 8$, 112 is not between these two numbers.

B. 2 and 3 $\quad$ $2^3 = 8$ and $3^3 = 27$, 112 is not between these two numbers.

C. 3 and 4 $\quad$ $3^3 = 27$ and $4^3 = 64$, 112 is not between these two numbers.

D. 4 and 5 $\quad$ $4^3 = 64$ and $5^3 = 125$, 112 is between these two numbers.

E. 5 and 6 $\quad$ $5^3 = 125$ and $6^3 = 126$, 112 is not between these two numbers.

30) Choice B is correct

15 second is one fourth of a minute. One fourth of 72 is 18. $72 \div 4 = 18$. Jack types 18 words in 15 seconds.

31) Choice D is correct

The amount of money that Jack earns for one hour: $\frac{\$616}{44} = \$14$

A number of additional hours that he works to make enough money is: $\frac{\$826-\$616}{1.5\times\$14} = 10$

Number of total hours is: $44 + 10 = 54$

32) Choice E is correct

In scientific notation all numbers are written in the form of: $m \times 10^n$, where m is between 1 and 10. To find an equivalent value of 0.000,000,000,000,042,121, move the decimal point to the right so that you have a number that is between 1 and 10. Then: 4.2121. Now, determine how many places the decimal moved in step 1, then put it as the power of 10. We moved the decimal point 14 places. Then: 10^{-14} when the decimal moved to the right, the exponent is negative.

Then: $0.000,000,000,000,042,121 = 4.2121 \times 10^{-14}$

33) Choice C is correct

A. $|4 - 2| = |2| = 2$

B. $|2 - 4| = |-2| = 2$

C. $|-2 - 4| = |-6| = 6$

D. $|2 - 4| - |4 - 2| = |2| - |2| = 2 - 2 = 0$

E. $|2 - 4| + |4 - 2| = |-2| + |2| = 2 + 2 = 4$

Choice C is the largest number.

34) Choice D is correct

85% of 40 is: $0.85 \times 40 = 34$. So, the student solves 34 questions correctly.

35) Choice B is correct

Use simple interest formula:

$I = prt$ ($I = interest, p = principal, r = rate, t = time$)

Simple interest $I = 2,500 \times 0.08 \times 6 = 1,200$

She will pay $1,200 interest at the end of 6 years.

36) Choice C is correct

Since integer x is evenly divisible by 4, substitute 4 for x in the answer choices to determine which expression is also divisible by 4: Let $x = 4$.

Choice A:	$x + 1 = 4 + 1 = 5$	This is NOT divisible by 4.
Choice B:	$2x + 1 = 2(4) + 1 = 9$	This is NOT divisible by 4.
Choice C:	$2x + 4 = 2(4) + 4 = 12$	This is divisible by 4.
Choice D:	$3x + 2 = 3(4) + 2 = 14$	This is NOT divisible by 4.
Choice E:	$4x + 1 = 4(4) + 1 = 17$	This is NOT divisible by 4.

So, choice C is correct.

37) Choice E is correct

Fist, find the length of the ribbon around the box, then add 10% of it.

$(8 \times 5) + (2 \times 20) + (6 \times 10) = 40 + 40 + 60 = 140 \; in$

10% of 140: $\frac{10}{100} \times 140 = \frac{1,400}{100} = 14 \; in$

$140 \; in + 14 \; in = 154 \; in$

38) Choice E is correct

There are currently 16 balls in the bag $(5 + 8 + 3)$. Of those balls, 11 are not blue. So, the probability of choosing a ball that is not blue is $\frac{11}{16}$.

39) Choice D is correct

First, calculate Jack's riding time in minutes: 1 hour 20 minutes = 80 minutes

Then, convert kilometers to meters: 160 kilometers = 160,000 meters

Now simplify the ratio to find the answer: $\frac{160,000}{80} = 2,000$ meters

40) Choice E is correct

If x is the smaller consecutive integer, then $x + 1$ is the larger consecutive integer. Use their sum (-13) to find x:

$$x + (x + 1) = -13 \rightarrow 2x + 1 = -13 \rightarrow 2x = -14 \rightarrow x = -7$$

The two consecutive integers are -7 and -6. 2 is added to the smaller integer:

$-7 + 2 = -5$, and 3 is subtracted from the larger integer: $-6 - 3 = -9$ find the product: $-5 \times (-9) = 45$

41) Choice D is correct

The two greatest integers less than -3.34 are -4 and -5. Since -5 is odd, the answer is -4.

42) Choice A is correct

$$(2)^3 + (-3)^2 + 2x - 6 = 11 \rightarrow 8 + 9 + 2x - 6 = 11$$

Combine like terms: $11 + 2x = 11 \rightarrow 2x = 0 \rightarrow x = 0$

43) Choice D is correct

The relationship among all sides of special right triangle

$30° - 60° - 90°$ is provided in this triangle:

In this triangle, the opposite side of $30°$ angle is half of the hypotenuse.

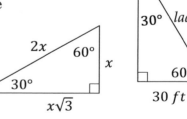

Draw the shape of this question:

The latter is the hypotenuse. Therefore, the latter is $60\ ft$.

44) Choice B is correct

$(6 - 1) \times 160 = 800$ centimeters

45) Choice D is correct

Plug in the values of x in the choices provided and check the answers.

A. $y = \frac{2}{3}x \rightarrow y = \frac{2}{3} \times (2) = \frac{2 \times 2}{3} = \frac{4}{3}$

B. $y = \frac{3}{2}x \rightarrow y = \frac{3}{2} \times (2) = \frac{3 \times 2}{2} = \frac{6}{2} = 3$

C. $y = 2(x - 1) \rightarrow y = 3(2 - 2) = 3(0) = 0$

D. $y = 3x - 1 \rightarrow y = 3(2) - 1 = 5$

E. $y = 4x - 2 \rightarrow y = 4(2) - 2 = 6$

Only Choice D is correct.

46) Choice D is correct

Let's find the mean (average), mode and median of the number of cities for each type of pollution. Number of cities for each type of pollution: $6, 3, 4, 9, 8$

$$average \ (mean) = \frac{sum \ of \ terms}{number \ of \ terms} = \frac{6 + 3 + 4 + 9 + 8}{5} = \frac{30}{5} = 6$$

The Median is the number in the middle. To find median, first list numbers in order from smallest to largest. $3, 4, 6, 8, 9$. The median of the data is 6.

Mode is the number which appears most often in a set of numbers. Therefore, there is no mode in the set of numbers. Median = Mean, then, $a = c$

47) Choice A is correct

Percent of cities in the type of pollution A: $\frac{6}{10} \times 100 = 60\%$

Percent of cities in the type of pollution C: $\frac{4}{10} \times 100 = 40\%$

Percent of cities in the type of pollution D: $\frac{9}{10} \times 100 = 90\%$

48) Choice A is correct

Let the number of cities should be added to type of pollutions B be x. Then:

$\frac{x+3}{8} = 0.625 \rightarrow x + 3 = 8 \times 0.625 \rightarrow x + 3 = 5 \rightarrow x = 2$

49) Choice C is correct

Let x be the missing number. Then:

$\$365.76 + \$289.55 + \$378.45 + \$289.99 + \$1,459 + x = \$3,332.49 \rightarrow$

$\$2,782.75 + x = \$3,332.49 \rightarrow x = \$3,332.49 - \$2,782.75 = \$549.74$

50) Choice B is correct

Use the average formula:

$$average \ (mean) = \frac{sum \ of \ terms}{number \ of \ terms} = \frac{9+12+15+16+19+16+14.5}{7} = 14.5$$

CBEST Mathematics Practice Test 4 explanations

1) Choice D is correct

The capacity of a red box is 20% bigger than the capacity of a blue box and it can hold 30 books. Therefore, we want to find a number that 20% bigger than that number is 30. Let x be that number. Then: $1.20 \times x = 30$. Divide both sides of the equation by 1.2. Then: $x = \frac{30}{1.20} = 25$

2) Choice C is correct

Convert everything into an equation: $35 = (3 \times \text{shirt}) - 10$

Now, solve the equation: $45 = 3\,\text{shirt} \rightarrow \text{shirt} = \frac{45}{3} = 15$. The price of the shirt was $15.

3) Choice E is correct

First, convert the improper fraction to a mixed number: $-\frac{32}{5} = -6\frac{2}{5}$

The two closest integers to this fraction are -7 and -6.

The integer less than $-\frac{32}{5}$ is -7.

4) Choice D is correct

Let x equal the smallest angle of the triangle. Then, the three angles are $x, 3x$, and $5x$. The sum of the angles of a triangle is 180. Set up an equation using this to find x:

$x + 3x + 5x = 180 \rightarrow 9x = 180 \rightarrow x = 20$

Since the question asks for the measure of the largest angle, $5x = 5(20) = 100°$

5) Choice E is correct

The angle $(2x - 5)$ and 55 are supplementary angles. Therefore:

$(2x - 5) + 55 = 180 \rightarrow 2x + 50 = 180 \rightarrow 2x = 180 - 50 \rightarrow 2x = 130 \rightarrow x = \frac{130}{2} \rightarrow x = 65$

6) Choice C is correct

There are 6 digits in the repeating decimal (0.142857), so digit 1 would be the first, seventh, thirteenth digit and so on. To find the 68th digit, divide 68 by 6.

$68 \div 6 = 11r2$

7) Choice C is correct

Based on triangle similarity theorem: $\frac{a}{a+b} = \frac{c}{3} \rightarrow c = \frac{3a}{a+b} = \frac{3\sqrt{3}}{3\sqrt{3}} = 1 \rightarrow$ Area of shaded region is: $\left(\frac{c+3}{2}\right)(b) = \frac{4}{2} \times 2\sqrt{3} = 4\sqrt{3}$

8) Choice A is correct

Two Angles are supplementary when they add up to 180 degrees.

$135° + 45° = 180°$

9) Choice B is correct

Use simple interest formula:

$I = prt$ ($I = interest$, $p = principal$, $r = rate$, $t = time$)

$I = prt \rightarrow 600 = (3,000)(0.05)(t) \rightarrow 600 = 150t \rightarrow t = 4$

10) Choice D is correct

Consider the case where $k = 1$

$n - k = 46 \rightarrow n - 1 = 46 \rightarrow n - 1 + 1 = 46 + 1 \rightarrow n = 47$

The list of integers from 1 to 47 contains 47 numbers.

11) Choice D is correct

To solve, add the two given fractions: $2\frac{2}{5} + 1\frac{3}{4}$

The common denominator is 20: $2\frac{8}{20} + 1\frac{15}{20} = 3\frac{23}{20} = 4\frac{3}{20}$

12) Choice E is correct

The original piece of paper is $2\frac{3}{5}$ feet long.

The shorter piece is x feet long, and it must be less than half the length of the original piece of paper. Since half of $2\frac{3}{5}$ is $1\frac{3}{10}$ it follows that $x < 1\frac{3}{10}$.

13) Choice A is correct

First, find the sum of course grade of Anna, $average = \frac{sum\ of\ terms}{number\ of\ terms} \Rightarrow$

$80 = \frac{sum\ of\ course\ grade}{5} \rightarrow the\ sum\ of\ course\ grade = 80 \times 5 = 400$

Anna and William have the same sum of course grade, now find the Williams mean

$$average = \frac{sum\ of\ course\ grade}{number\ of\ course} \Rightarrow \frac{400}{8} = 50$$

14) Choice D is correct

List in order the odd numbers between 5 to 30: $7, 9, 11, 13, 15, 17, 19, 21, 23, 25, 27,$ and 29. Since, the numbers are consecutive odd numbers, the mean and the median are equal. The median is the number in the middle. Since we have 12 numbers, the median is the average of numbers 6 and 7 which are 17 and 19. The mean (or the median) is: Mean $= \frac{17+19}{2} = 18$

15) Choice B is correct

60% of students can't swim→ $100 - 60 = 40\%$ can swim.

Then: $0.40 \times 45 = 18$

16) Choice D is correct

Money received by 14 person = \$8,400. So, the money received by one person is:

$\frac{\$8,400}{14} = \$600$

17) Choice A is correct

There are 12 sticks in the box $(6 + 4 + 2)$. So, the probability that Emma picks a green stick is: $Probability = \frac{6}{12} = \frac{1}{2}$

18) Choice B is correct

Use the percent increase expression to find the answer:

$\frac{new\ price-original\ price}{original\ price} = \frac{5.67-5.40}{5.40} = 0.05 = 5\%$

19) Choice C is correct

Let x be the number of blue marbles. Write the items in the ratio as a fraction:

$\frac{x}{150} = \frac{4}{3} \rightarrow 3x = 600 \rightarrow x = 200$

20) Choice A is correct

Let x be the number: $\frac{5}{8}x = 90 \rightarrow x = 90 \times \frac{8}{5} = \frac{720}{5} = 144$

21) Choice E is correct

Set up a proportion to solve: $\frac{\frac{5}{14} \, cherry}{\frac{5}{70} \, apple} = \frac{x \, cherry}{1 \, apple} \rightarrow \frac{5}{14} \times \frac{70}{5} = x \rightarrow x = \frac{70}{14} = \frac{10}{2} \rightarrow x = 5$

22) Choice D is correct

$2m = n + 5 \rightarrow m = \frac{n+5}{2}$. Substitute each value of n to find the values of m:

$$m = \frac{5+5}{2} = \frac{10}{2} = 5$$

$$m = \frac{3+5}{2} = \frac{8}{2} = 4$$

$$m = \frac{7+5}{2} = \frac{12}{2} = 6$$

The set of m is {5,4,6}.

23) Choice B is correct

Plug in 25 for x in the equation.

A. $x + 10 = 40 \rightarrow 25 + 10 \neq 40$

B. $4x = 100 \rightarrow 4(25) = 100$

C. $3x = 70 \rightarrow 3(25) \neq 70$

D. $\frac{x}{2} = 12 \rightarrow \frac{25}{2} \neq 12$

E. $\frac{x}{3} = 8 \rightarrow \frac{25}{3} \neq 8$

Only choice B is correct.

24) Choice D is correct

Jack scored a mean of 80 per test. In the first 4 tests, the sum of scores is:

$80 \times 4 = 320$. Now, calculate the mean over the 5 tests: $\frac{320+90}{5} = \frac{410}{5} = 82$

25) Choice A is correct

Volume of the cube is less than $64 \, m^3$. Use the formula of volume of cubes.

$Volume = (one \, side)^3 \Rightarrow 64 = (one \, side)^3$. Find the cube root of both sides.

$64 = (one\ side)^3 \rightarrow one\ side = \sqrt[3]{64} = 4\ m$

Then: $4 = $ one side. The side of the cube is less than 4. Only choice A is less than 4.

26) Choice B is correct

First draw an isosceles triangle. Remember that two legs of the triangle are equal.

Let put a for the legs. Then:

$a = 6 \Rightarrow$ Area of the triangle is $= \frac{1}{2}(6 \times 6) = \frac{36}{2} = 18\ cm^2$

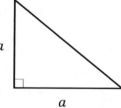

27) Choice C is correct

Solve for x: $0.00104 = \frac{104}{x}$, multiply both sides by x, $(0.00104)(x) = \frac{104}{x}(x)$.

Simplify: $0.00104x = 104$. Divide both side by 0.00104: $\frac{0.00104x}{0.00104} = \frac{104}{0.00104}$, simplify

$x = \frac{104}{0.00104} = 100{,}000$

28) Choice E is correct

The number of cards in the bag is 15.

$Probability = \frac{number\ of\ desired\ outcomes}{number\ of\ total\ outcomes} = \frac{1}{15}$

29) Choice D is correct

$(2x + 4)°$ and $96°$ are vertical angles. Vertical angles are equal in measure.

Then: $2x + 4 = 96 \rightarrow 2x = 92 \rightarrow x = 46$

30) Choice B is correct

The two-digit numbers must be even, so the only possible two-digit numbers must end in 6, since 6 is the only even digit given in the problem. Since the numbers cannot be repeated, the only possibilities for two-digit even numbers are 76 and 56. Thus, the answer is two possible two-digit numbers.

31) Choice A is correct

First convert 24 inches to feet. 12 inch $=$ 1 feet, thus: $24 \div 12 = 2\ feet$. Then, calculate the volume, in cubic feet: $25 \times 6 \times 2 = 300\ ft^3$

32) Choice D is correct

First calculate exponents value, then multiplying and subtracting:

$200(3 + 0.01)^2 - 200 = 200(3.01)^2 - 200 = 200(9.0601) - 200 = 1,612.02$

33) Choice C is correct

Since 90 boxes contain 360 kg vegetable. Therefore, 1 box contains $\frac{360\,kg}{90} = 4\,kg$ vegetable.

34) Choice C is correct

Let n represent a number in the sequence, and let x represent the number that comes just before n. $n = 4 + 2x \rightarrow 84 = 4 + 2x \rightarrow 80 = 2x \rightarrow x = 40$

35) Choice C is correct

Use PEMDAS (order of operation): $[6 \times (-24) + 8] - (-4) + [4 \times 5] \div 2 =$

$[-144 + 8] - (-4) + [20] \div 2 = [-144 + 8] + 4 + 10 = [-136] + 4 + 10 = -122$

36) Choice D is correct

Perimeter of rectangle is equal to the sum of all the sides of the rectangle:

Perimeter $= 2(14) + 2(5) = 28 + 10 = 38\,cm$

37) Choice D is correct

$3\frac{1}{4} + 2\frac{4}{16} + 1\frac{3}{8} + 5\frac{1}{2}$. Convert all the fractions to a common denominator (16):

$3\frac{4}{16} + 2\frac{4}{16} + 1\frac{6}{16} + 5\frac{8}{16} = (3 + 2 + 1 + 5) + \left(\frac{4+4+6+8}{16}\right) = 11 + 1\frac{6}{16} = 12\frac{6}{16} = 12\frac{3}{8}$

38) Choice A is correct

One gram is equal to 1,000 milligrams, or 1 milligram is equal to $\frac{1}{1,000}$ gram.

Thus, 85 milligrams $= \frac{85}{1,000} = 0.085$ gram

39) Choice E is correct

Check each choice provided:

A. 1 $\frac{4+5+8+11+12}{5} = \frac{40}{5} = 8$

B. 4 $\frac{1+5+8+11+12}{5} = \frac{37}{5} = 7.4$

C. 5 $\frac{1+4+8+11+12}{5} = \frac{36}{5} = 7.2$

D. 8 $\frac{1+4+5+11+12}{5} = \frac{33}{5} = 6.6$

E. 11 $\frac{1+4+5+8+12}{5} = \frac{30}{5} = 6$

40) Choice E is correct

Substitute 6 for m and -3 for n:

$$\frac{5-9(3+n)}{3m-5(2-n)} = \frac{5-9(3+(-3))}{3(6)-5(2-(-3))} = \frac{5-9(0)}{18-5(5)} = \frac{5}{18-25} = \frac{5}{-7} = -\frac{5}{7}$$

41) Choice B is correct

To answer this question, we need to divide 28 by 7: $\frac{28}{7} = 4$

42) Choice B is correct

Simple interest (y) is calculated by multiplying the initial deposit (p), by the interest rate (r), and time (t). $360 = 240 \times 0.10 \times t \rightarrow 360 = 24t \rightarrow t = \frac{360}{24} = 15$

So, it takes 15 years to get $360 with an investment of $240.

43) Choice C is correct

There are 60 minutes in 1 hour. Divide the number of minutes by the number of minutes in 1 hour: $\frac{1,800}{60} = 30$ hours

44) Choice B is correct

First calculate absolute values: $|-44| - x + |8| = 36 \rightarrow 44 - x + 8 = 36$

Combine like terms: $44 + 8 - 36 = x \rightarrow x = 16$

45) Choice D is correct

According to the figure above, the length of each side of a small square is 2 units. First, count the number of units around the shaded part. The number of sides all around the shaded part is 30. So the total length of the fence needed is $2 \times 30 = 60$.

46) Choice B is correct

$900 - 700 = 200$

47) Choice D is correct

Use the percent increase formula to find the answer:

$$Percent\ change = \frac{New\ Value - Old\ Value}{Old\ Value} \times 100\% \Rightarrow \frac{2,183 - 1,850}{1,850} \times 100\% = 18\%$$

48) Choice D is correct

$$Average = \frac{sum\ of\ data}{number\ of\ data} = \frac{1,600+1,200+1,400+1,800+1,900+1,700+1,600}{7} = \frac{11,200}{7} = 1,600$$

49) Choice A is correct

$$Average = \frac{sum\ of\ data}{number\ of\ data}$$

$$James\ Average = \frac{(1,000+2,000+3,500+2,500+3,000+2,000+3,500)}{7} = \frac{17,500}{7} = 2,500\ meter$$

$$John\ Average = \frac{(2,000+3,000+1,000+1,500+2,500+3,000+1,000)}{7} = \frac{14,000}{7} = 2,000\ meter$$

$$Difference\ average = James\ Average - John\ Average = 2,500 - 2,000 = 500\ meter$$

50) Choice E is correct

Maximum distance James = 3,500 meter

Minimum distance James = 1,000 meter

3,500 − 1,000 = 2,500 meter

CBEST Mathematics Practice Test 5 Explanations

1) Choice A is correct

First, find the sale price. 15% of $45.00 is $6.75, so the sale price is

$45.00 − $6.75 = $38.25. Next, find the price after Nick's employee discount. 20% × $38.25 = $7.65, so, the final price of the shoes is $38.25 − $7.65 = $30.60.

2) Choice B is correct

Let's compare the fractions by converting them to decimals:

A. $\frac{2}{5} = 0.4$

B. $\frac{3}{4} = 0.75$

C. $\frac{6}{10} = 0.6$

D. $\frac{3}{5} = 0.6$

E. $\frac{7}{8} = 0.875$

Only 0.75 can be entered in the box.

$\frac{5}{8} < \square < \frac{4}{5} \rightarrow 0.625 < \square < 0.8 \rightarrow 0.625 < 0.75 < 0.8$

3) Choice A is correct

The total number of possible sections in the spinner = 10

There are two sections containing Number D. Then, the probability of spinning a D is: $\frac{2}{10} = \frac{1}{5}$

4) Choice B is correct

The factors of 45 are: { 1, 3, 5, 9, 15, 45}. Only choice B is correct.

5) Choice D is correct

$Percent\ of\ change = \frac{new\ number - original\ number}{original\ number} = \frac{18.36 - 15.30}{15.30} = 20\%$

6) Choice B is correct

First find the multiples of 8 that fall between 10 and 60: 16, 24, 32, 40, 48, 56. Since the greatest common factor of 32 and x is 8, x cannot be 32 (otherwise the GCF would be 32, not 8). There are 5 remaining values: 16, 24, 40, 48 and 56. Number 16 is also not possible (otherwise the GCF would be 16, not 8). Then, there are 4 possible values for x.

7) Choice C is correct

The total number of candies in the box is $6 + 4 + 3 = 13$. The number of candies that are not orange is $6 + 3 = 9$. The probability of the first candy not being orange is $\frac{9}{13}$. Now, out of 12 candies, there are 8 candies left that are not orange. The probability of the second candy not being orange is $\frac{8}{12}$. Multiply these two probabilities to get the solution: $\frac{9}{13} \times \frac{8}{12} = \frac{72}{156} = \frac{24}{52} = \frac{6}{13}$

8) Choice B is correct

First, change the improper fractions into mixed numbers: $\frac{7}{2} = 3\frac{1}{2}$ and $\frac{30}{4} = 7\frac{1}{2}$

The integers between these two values are 4, 5, 6 and 7. So, there are 4 integers between $\frac{7}{5}$ and $\frac{30}{4}$.

9) Choice C is correct

The increase in sales tax percentage is $8.5\% - 8.0\% = 0.5\%$

0.5% of $250 is $(0.5\%)(250) = (0.005)(250) = 1.25\$$

10) Choice C is correct

When a point is reflected over x axes, the (y) coordinate of that point changes to $(-y)$ while its x coordinate remains the same. $C(7, 9) \rightarrow C'(7, -9)$

11) Choice B is correct

First, list the products:

$1 \times 4 = 4$	$4 \times 5 = 20$
$1 \times 6 = 6$	$4 \times 7 = 28$
$1 \times 5 = 5$	$6 \times 5 = 30$
$1 \times 7 = 7$	$6 \times 7 = 42$
$4 \times 6 = 24$	$5 \times 7 = 35$

Out of 10 results, 3 numbers are odd. The answer is: $\frac{3}{10}$

12) Choice C is correct

Since $5n$ is even, then $5n + 1$ must be odd. Thus $5n + 3$ and $5n + 5$ are also odd. So, there are a total of 3 numbers in this range that are odd.

13) Choice B is correct

The height of the building is 4 units.

$2,760 \; centimeters \div 4 = 690 \; centimeters$

14) Choice C is correct

First, use the given information to calculate the value of a: $\frac{a}{4} = b \rightarrow \frac{a}{4} = 2 \rightarrow a = 8$

Now, calculate $a^2 + 4b$ by substituting $a = 8$ and $b = 2$, $(8)^2 + 4(2) = 72$

15) Choice A is correct

Since 0.0099 is equal to 0.99%, the closest to that value is 0.1%.

16) Choice C is correct

Surface Area of a cylinder $= 2\pi r(r + h)$, The radius of the cylinder is 3 $(6 \div 2)$ inches and its height is 8 inches.

Therefore, Surface Area of a cylinder $= 2\pi(3)(3 + 8) = 66\pi \; in^2$

17) Choice C is correct

First, find the speed of the train in miles per hour: $280 \div 4 = 70$ miles per hour

The number of miles left to travel is: $1,500 - 280 = 1,220$ miles

To find the number of hours left, use the equation

$d = rt \rightarrow (distance) = (rate) \times (time) \rightarrow 1,220 = 70t$

$t = \frac{1,220}{70} = 17.4285714$ hours. That number rounded to the nearest whole hour is 17 hours.

18) Choice B is correct

Let x be the original price. Then:

$$\$1{,}912.50 = x - 0.15(x) \rightarrow 1{,}912.50 = 0.85x \rightarrow x = \frac{1{,}912.50}{0.85} \rightarrow x = 2{,}250$$

19) Choice C is correct

Let x be the number of inches representing 2.5 feet. Set up a proportion and solve for x: $\frac{x}{2.5} = \frac{0.15}{150} \rightarrow x = \frac{0.15 \times 2.5}{150} \rightarrow x = 0.0025\ in$

20) Choice D is correct

Set an equation: $\frac{3}{7}Z = 54$

Solve for Z: $\rightarrow Z = 54 \times \frac{7}{3} = 126,$ then, calculate $\frac{2}{5}Z$: $\frac{2}{5} \times 126 = 50.4$

21) Choice A is correct

To answer this question, multiply 72 miles per hour to $8 \rightarrow 72 \times 8 = 576$ miles

22) Choice D is correct

The spent amount is \$60, and the tip is 25%. Then: $tip = 0.25 \times 60 = \$15$

Final price = Selling price+tip $\rightarrow$ final price = $\$60 + \$15 = \$75$

23) Choice E is correct

To find the smallest factor of 95, list the factors: $1, 5, 19,$ and $95.$ The smallest factor (other than 1) is 5. Of the choices listed $(28, 32, 39,$ and $45),$ only 45 is a multiple of 5.

24) Choice A is correct

Adding exponents is done by calculating each exponent first and then adding and dividing:

$$\frac{4^2 + 3^2 + (-5)^2}{(9 + 10 - 11)^2} = \frac{16 + 9 + 25}{(8)^2} = \frac{50}{64} = \frac{25}{32}$$

25) Choice B is correct

Angle A and angle B are supplementary, so the sum of their angles is $180°$.

Let a equal the measure of angle A, and let b equal the measure of angle B.

$a + b = 180$

The measure of angle A is 2 times the measure of angle B.

$$a = 2b \rightarrow 2b + b = 180 \rightarrow 3b = 180 \rightarrow b = \frac{180}{3} = 60$$

$$a = 2b = 2(60) = 120$$

Therefore, the measure of angle A is $120°$.

26) Choice D is correct

First, convert their heights from feet and inches to inches, by multiplying the number of feet by 12 and adding the inches. Tomas:

6 feet $+8.5$ inches. $6(12$ inches$) +8.5$ inches $= 72$ inches $+8.5$ inches $= 80.5$ inches

Alex: 5 feet $+3$ inches. $5(12$ inches$)+3$ inches $= 60$ inches $+3$ inches $= 63$ inches

Then, subtract Alex's height from Tomas's height: $80.5 - 63 = 17.5$

27) Choice D is correct

So far, Kylie has written $10\% + 18\% = 28\%$ of the entire homework. That means she has $100\% - 28\% = 72\%$ left to write. $72\% = \frac{72}{100} = \frac{18}{25}$

28) Choice E is correct

Let x be the number of yellow pens. Write a proportion and solve: $\frac{yellow}{blue} = \frac{2}{3} = \frac{x}{9}$

Solve the equation: $18 = 3x \rightarrow x = 6$

29) Choice B is correct

To find the decimal equivalent to $-\frac{6}{9}$, divide 6 by 9. Then: $-\frac{6}{9} = -0.66666\ldots = -0.\overline{6}$

30) Choice E is correct

The formula for the area of the circle is πr^2, The area is 81π. Therefore:

$A = \pi r^2 \Rightarrow 81\pi = \pi r^2$, Divide both sides by π: $81 = r^2 \Rightarrow r = 9$, Diameter of a circle is $2 \times radius$. Then: $Diameter = 2 \times 9 = 18$

31) Choice E is correct

Five years ago, Amy was three times as old as Mike. Mike is 10 years now. Therefore, 5 years ago Mike was 5 years. Five years ago, Amy was: $A = 3 \times 5 = 15$, Now Amy is 20 years old: $15 + 5 = 20$

32) Choice B is correct

List the factors of 68: 1 and 68, 2 and 34, 4 and 17. There is one factor greater than 26 and less than 60.

33) Choice B is correct

Let the lengths of two sides of the parallelogram be $2x\ cm$ and $3x\ cm$ respectively. Then, its perimeter $= 2(2x + 3x) = 10x$

Therefore, $10x = 40 \rightarrow x = 4$

One side $= 2(4) = 8\ cm$ and other side is: $3(4) = 12\ cm$

34) Choice E is correct

Isolate x in the equation and solve. Then:

$\frac{3}{4}(x - 2) = 3\left(\frac{1}{6}x - \frac{3}{2}\right)$, expand $\frac{3}{4}$ and 3 to the parentheses $\rightarrow \frac{3}{4}x - \frac{3}{2} = \frac{1}{2}x - \frac{9}{2}$. Add $\frac{3}{2}$ to both sides: $\frac{3}{4}x - \frac{3}{2} + \frac{3}{2} = \frac{1}{2}x - \frac{9}{2} + \frac{3}{2}$. Simplify: $\frac{3}{4}x = \frac{1}{2}x - 3$. Now, subtract $\frac{1}{2}x$ from both sides: $\frac{3}{4}x - \frac{1}{2}x = \frac{1}{2}x - 3 - \frac{1}{2}x$. Simplify: $\frac{1}{4}x = -3$. Multiply both sides by 4:

$(4)\frac{1}{4}x = -3(4)$, simplify $x = -12$

35) Choice C is correct

To answer this question, assign several positive and negative values to x and determine what the value of the expression will be:

x	-1	0	2	3	4
$2-x^2$	1	2	-2	-7	-14

So, the maximum value of the expression is 2.

36) Choice C is correct

The total number of handballs in the container is $6 + 5 + 8 + 10 = 29$. Since there are 6 green handballs, the probability of selecting a green handball is $\frac{6}{29}$.

37) Choice D is correct

If Emma answered 9 out of 45 questions incorrectly, then she answered 36 questions correctly. $\frac{36}{45} \times 100 = 80\%$

38) Choice C is correct

Let x be the number. Write the equation and solve for x.

30% of $x = 12 \Rightarrow 0.30x = 12 \Rightarrow x = 12 \div 0.30 = 40$

39) Choice A is correct

Let y be Anna's age: $5y + 3 = x \rightarrow 5y = x - 3 \rightarrow y = \frac{x-3}{5}$

40) Choice B is correct

The area of a trapezoid can be determined using the formula: $A = \frac{1}{2} \times (a + b) \times h$

We know: $DC = 4\ cm$, $AE = 2\ cm$, and $AD = 4\ cm \rightarrow$

$A = \frac{1}{2} \times (4\ cm + 2\ cm) \times 4\ cm = 12\ cm^2$

41) Choice E is correct

From the choices provided, only 0.061 is between 0.0048 and 0.069.

42) Choice C is correct

The reciprocal of $\frac{3}{5}$ is added to the reciprocal of $\frac{1}{4}$:

$\frac{4}{1} + \frac{5}{3} = \frac{12}{3} + \frac{5}{3} = \frac{17}{3}$. The reciprocal of this sum is $\frac{3}{17}$.

43) Choice D is correct

To eliminate the decimals in this equation, multiply the numerators and denominators by 100:

$\left(\frac{0.02}{0.25}\right)\left(\frac{100}{100}\right) = \left(\frac{1.25}{x}\right)\left(\frac{100}{100}\right) \rightarrow \left(\frac{2}{25}\right) = \frac{125}{100x} \rightarrow x = \left(\frac{125}{100}\right)\left(\frac{25}{2}\right) = 15.625$

44) Choice D is correct

From the choices provided, number -0.0028 is greater than 0.0029

45) Choice D is correct

1 pound = 16 ounces

1 pan = $(3 \times 16) + 8 = 56$ ounces. Now, convert ounces to pounds:

$56 \div 16 = 3.5$ pounds. Then: 5 pans = $(5 \times 3.5) = 17.5$ pounds

17.5 pounds = 17 pounds and $(0.5 \times 16) = 8$ ounces

46) Choice E is correct

According to the chart, grade 5 has the least number of girl students.

Grade 1 : 16 boys, 18 girls

Grade 2 : 14 boys, 16 girls

Grade 3 : 20 boys, 18 girls

Grade 4 : 17 boys, 20 girls

Grade 5 : 18 boys, 14 girls

47) Choice A is correct

Use the percent increase expression to find the answer:

$$Percent\ change = \frac{New\ Value - Old\ Value}{Old\ Value} \times 100\% \Rightarrow \frac{400-250}{250} \times 100\% = 60\%$$

48) Choice C is correct

Between 1990 and 2000, the number of car sales increased by 40,000 $(100,000 - 60,000)$.

49) Choice D is correct

To find the $200,000 + 500,000 + 250,000 + 150,000 = 1,100,000$

50) Choice E is correct

SUV revenue in 2000: $\$850,000 \times \frac{16}{100} = \frac{1,360,000}{100} = \$136,000$

SUV revenue in 2006: $980,000 \times \frac{20}{100} = \frac{1,960,000}{100} = \$196,000$

$\$196,000 - \$136,000 = \$60,000$

Effortless Math's CBEST Online Center

... So Much More Online!

Effortless Math Online CBEST Math Center offers a complete study program, including the following:

- ✓ Step-by-step instructions on how to prepare for the CBEST Math test

- ✓ Numerous CBEST Math worksheets to help you measure your math skills

- ✓ Complete list of CBEST Math formulas

- ✓ Video lessons for CBEST Math topics

- ✓ Full-length CBEST Math practice tests

- ✓ And much more...

No Registration Required.

Visit **EffortlessMath.com/CBEST** to find your online CBEST Math resources.

Receive the PDF version of this book or get another FREE book!

Thank you for using our Book!

Do you LOVE this book?

Then, you can get the PDF version of this book or another book absolutely FREE!

Please email us at:

info@EffortlessMath.com

for details.

Author's Final Note

I hope you enjoyed reading this book. You've made it through the book! Great job!

First of all, thank you for purchasing this practice book. I know you could have picked any number of books to help you prepare for your CBEST Math test, but you picked this book and for that I am extremely grateful.

It took me years to write this practice book for the CBEST Math because I wanted to prepare a comprehensive CBEST Math book to help test takers make the most effective use of their valuable time while preparing for the test.

After teaching and tutoring math courses for over a decade, I've gathered my personal notes and lessons to develop this practice test. It is my greatest hope that the practice tests in this book could help you prepare for your test successfully.

If you have any questions, please contact me at reza@effortlessmath.com and I will be glad to assist. Your feedback will help me to greatly improve the quality of my books in the future and make this book even better. Furthermore, I expect that I have made a few minor errors somewhere in this book. If you think this to be the case, please let me know so I can fix the issue as soon as possible.

If you enjoyed this book and found some benefit in reading this, I'd like to hear from you and hope that you could take a quick minute to post a review on the book's Amazon page. To leave your valuable feedback, please visit: amzn.to/3wgZkd0

Or scan this QR code.

I personally go over every single review, to make sure my books really are reaching out and helping students and test takers. Please help me help CBEST Math test takers, by leaving a review!

I wish you all the best in your future success!

Reza Nazari

Math teacher and author